KU-783-609

What God hath Wrought

The Story of The YMCA Inverness
1859-1992

By Edward Duncan Hughes

FOREWORD BY REV. WILLIAM STILL

129 Pennyland Drive
Thurso
Caithness
KW14 7QD
Tel. 01847 894091

COVER: By kind permission of the Inverness Museum and Art Gallery.

Our grateful thanks to the "Inverness Courier" for permission to quote.

Contents

Foreword
Author's Introduction

Foreword
by
William Still

My first impression on reading this history was of the quality of the writing, by a former Inverness YMCA boy. This impression was sustained to the end; it is, indeed, a typical example of the quality of life and work of the godly in the Highlands, perhaps maintained as well by successive generations of 'ordinary' YMCA boys, as by any who went before. For in a country whose religious history is as chequered by division as ours, the rich inter-denominational character of the Inverness YMCA, from its inception, and during all the time I have known it, is nothing less than phenomenal.

I could expatiate on this, as on other features of this God-blessed branch of Christ's Church (using the word "Church" advisedly although it is not a sacramental body); for if ever I have known a band of loving brothers in Christ, it is that of the Inverness YMCA.

However, necessity demands I be brief. The first decades of this work, despite its struggles, showed a remarkable degree of spiritual life and of godliness; but I notice, that after the 1859 revival and the Moody peak, when the church in Scotland began to question herself and her faith, there was a lull. And while faithful men kept the Association going all the way through the years, there was distinct loss of the vision of the earlier years. Like many in the churches in the latter years of the 1900's and into the 20th century, a new worldliness tended to creep in, to mar and spoil, and cause deep questions to be asked by the godly as to the trends.

Then came the First World War which, although it afforded

opportunity for the YMCA to perform valiant service with the troops in the area, nonetheless led to spiritual decline, which, alas, was typical of the state of Christianity in general in Scotland during the first 20 to 30 years of this century. It was not until a young man, converted in Jerusalem through that outstanding evangelist, S. F. Cupples, was demobilised that the work of the Inverness YMCA took a turn for the better and got off to such a start as has carried it through many decades since. This young man's name was Tom MacDonald. Nor is there any doubt that the history of Inverness YMCA thereafter is dominated by that one man whom I have often characterised as an absolutely unique force for evangelism in Scotland. This record, from that time onwards, is practically one of what the Lord did through this man. I, for one, am proud to own it. I must therefore be allowed to say a word about him.

Rugged to the core, Tom MacDonald had a drive and determination about him such as I have not known in any man, with, perhaps, the solitary exception of Billy Graham. And yet, what endeared him to me, and helped form a bond of mutual regard and affection between us which I have found to be rare in a long life, was that under that bluff exterior and driving force, there was not only the kindest and gentlest heart; but hidden, deep down in his personality, something of an inward anguish such as I myself have known, and which makes us nothing less than blood brothers!

There are few that I admire as I do Tom. I salute him with every fibre of my being, not least because in days when I was in the throes of strife, with almost intolerable tensions arising from the work in Aberdeen, I had simply to jump into my car and arrive at the door of Inverness YMCA to be received with such a unique brand of kindness as did more to comfort and encourage me than anything else in the world.

I can never forget what I owe to you, Tom, and your boys. Dear Wilf, thank you for the innumerable cups of tea made by your hand in that lounge as I sat speaking to these wonderful lads until two or three in the morning before I repaired to my little caravan on Loch Ness side; how could I ever thank you.

This is a formidable record; and I will gladly put it on our bookstall when it is published, and recommend it far and wide as a series of lessons on how to serve God; which is perhaps unrivalled in its period in Scotland and perhaps much further afield.

Rev. William Still
Aberdeen, Scotland.
October 10, 1992.

Other Titles by the Author:
"Night Duty — Social Worker"
"Love Them For Me Laura"
"See What God Has Done"
"Three Loves"

Published by YMCA, Bank Street, Inverness

Printed by Highland Printers, Henderson Road, Inverness

Author's Introduction

For over thirty years, I've lived in Winnipeg, Canada, far from the banks of the River Ness and the hallowed halls of Inverness YMCA. Yet, the influence of that institution, because it helped set the foundation, has also shaped the form of my whole adult life. In those halls I was first taught the grand truths of God's Word. Through those halls, my life intertwined with other young Christians in a fellowship which became deep and lasting. From those halls I, with my brothers in Christ, went out to our world, the town of Inverness, to witness to the saving Grace and keeping power of the Lord Jesus Christ.

I was a boy then. Now, I am a man, in the reflective stage of my earthly pilgrimage. I acknowledge that Time's tides have changed the patterns on the sands of my life's shore. Amongst the things which have remained constant, however, are my awareness of how God used Inverness YMCA, my appreciation of the friends I made there.

Space does not permit me to name all of these friends. I name only one, because that one became to me a model of practical Christian living - even radical Christian living. He was there in 1957 on the night I entered into new life through personal faith in the Lord Jesus Christ. He has been there ever since as my friend and mentor. His name is Tom MacDonald. His incomparable record of loving ministry speaks for itself in the pages which follow. His motto, included on all the YMCA handbills, has been incorporated into my life. It comes from a well-known hymn

On Christ, the solid rock I stand
All other ground is sinking sand.

I thank everybody in Inverness who helped me write this account; amd I especially acknowledge and thank my dear wife, Helen, whose eagle eye caught many a mistake in the proofing, and whose gentle spirit unconsciously modified my expression.

I accept the gracious forgiveness of those whose names I have inadvertently failed to include, or whom I have represented inadequately. Responsibility for any mistakes are mine alone. The records on high carry no mistakes - and no names are forgotten.

Edward D. Hughes
Winnipeg, 1992.

Chapter One

A Tragic Accident

Jumping off his regulation-red bicycle young Telegraph Boy Wilfred Urquhart hurried into the Post Office. In the middle of a busy Saturday shift, he expected to pick up more telegrams for delivery. Instead, his foreman met him with averted gaze. "You're to go to the Post Master's office right away!" Mystified, Wilfred did as he was told.

"I want you to sign off duty immediately and go to your Aunt's house," the Post Master ordered.

On his way up the hill to his Aunt's house, Wilf pondered the strange circumstances. A country boy who originally came to Inverness as a high school student and now dwelt in a dormitory-type rooming establishment with other young working lads, Wilf could not guess why he should go to his Aunt's house. His parents lived near Fort William. Right now his brother Robert, who worked in the same department as Wilf, was enjoying holidays with the family at home.

Wilf himself had badgered the boss to let him have holidays too. But department policy forbade more than one employee being away at any one time. Robert, being senior, had the first choice. Wilf could only submit to department policy and envy his brother the time of family fellowship he himself had to miss. Why, even Aunt Ina from Southern Scotland was visiting the Urquhart home, having come to help celebrate the wedding of William, Wilf's oldest brother. The Urquharts had hired a motor car for the occasion, which had taken place only the previous Saturday. They held the hired car over because

Robert, home on holiday for the week following the wedding, was available to drive his parents and Aunt around the beautiful Highlands of Scotland.

Wilf and Robert got on well together. Only a year and a half separated them in age, and working in the same Post Office department tended to keep them close. For some months previously, Robert persisted in inviting Wilfred to accompany him to church and to Inverness YMCA but Wilf wasn't interested.

Not a rowdy boy, Wilf had a consuming interest in movies and went to the cinema every evening except Sunday. There were three picture houses in the Inverness of the late 1950's, the La Scala, the Palace and the Playhouse. Each of them changed their show in mid-week. That suited Wilf perfectly. Week after week, month after month, Wilfred went to the "pictures" six times a week. Afternoon free time and Sundays saw him enjoy his one other major interest, cycling.

"I remember thinking it strange that Robert should invite me to church," Wilfred was to later recall. "He had been converted to Christ in the YMCA, and I did see a definite change in his life. But it wasn't for me."

When Wilfred arrived at his Aunt and Uncle's house he had no more insight into the situation than when he set out from the Post Master's office. But Wilfred did notice the solemn expression on his Aunt's face. Seating him down, Wilfred's uncle thrust a drink into the boy's hand, even though Wilf had never been even a moderate drinker. Then his Aunt gave him the news.

"Robert's had an accident." Wilf's Aunt paused to control her trembling voice. "The car went through a canal gate into the water. Your mother and father and Aunt Ina were with Robert in the car. None of them..." It wasn't necessary for her to finish. Wilf's ashen face and stunned expression showed all too clearly that his mind had comprehended his Aunt's meaning, even though his emotions were anesthetized with shock. He sat there motionless, his eyes fixed on his Aunt as she told him the details.

"A bus was parked on a bend just at the loch gates. Maybe Robert thought the driver was picking up passengers. He overtook the bus, but couldn't stop when he saw that a ship was going through the canal and the bridge barrier was up. The car went over, hit the ship and disappeared in the waters." Perhaps there was some relief for Wilf's Aunt in laying out the details so specifically. Perhaps that process helped her to come to grips in some way with the awful horror of the tragedy. Wilf made no response as she continued. "It was a training ship with naval divers. They were already in gear and went down instantly. When they finally located the car, it was too late."

In total emotional numbness, Wilf passively acquiesced when his uncle informed him that they would drive as it was necessary for Wilf to go to Royal Northern Infirmary to identify the accident victims. Accident victims! His mother, his father, his brother, his Aunt Ina. Zombie-like, he stared through the car windshield, seeing nothing. At the Infirmary he walked heavy-footed to the door, only to be stopped by a policeman.

"How old are you, son?" The policeman stood guard outside the room containing the four bodies.

"Sixteen and a half," Wilfred replied woodenly.

"You can't go in here." Barring Wilfred entrance, the policeman made arrangements for the boy's Uncle to do what was necessary. Wilf was returned to the car, where he sat sphinx-like, his mind struggling to face the implications of the dreadful calamity which had come to him.

"Suddenly, the dam burst." Years later, Wilf was able to talk about it without breaking down. "I started to cry. My parents were gone. My brother, my Aunt Ina. I can't explain how void of meaning this world suddenly became. It was then I decided to commit suicide. Waiting in the car, I worked out exactly how I was going to end my life."

Wilf's plan was simple. The River Ness, across which Wilf had to cross each day to reach his lodgings, was in full spate following an extended period of unusually rainy weather. Wilf determined that he would step into the river at the Greig Street bridge and end an existence which so suddenly had lost all reason for being. There was no question in his mind that he wanted to kill himself. And there was no lack of resolve in his determination to do it.

"Unwittingly, my Uncle foiled my plan by walking me all the way home uninvited," Wilf later divulged. "I wanted to get rid of him so I could do it, but it didn't happen."

In light of Wilf's strong resolution to commit suicide, it is remarkable that the temptation to do so never again entered his mind after that night. Traumatised with sadness and inward pain, he knew little of the difficulties his Uncle experienced in trying to track down William on honeymoon in London. His Uncle also made the funeral arrangements. The service, on June 17, 1958, was held in an Inverness funeral home chapel, and interment was at Tomnahurich Cemetery. Wilfred recollects trudging behind the two hearses, each carrying a double load. "I locked my gaze on these coffins and couldn't take it in that it was really happening," Wilf remembers. "Yet, the little detail sticks in my mind that every intersection was patrolled by a uniformed policeman and each one took off his hat and saluted as the cortege passed by."

After the accident, life changed drastically for Wilf. Outwardly, he continued to give good service at the Post Office. But the movies, the cycling, nothing of what had filled his life before now appealed to him. There was no solace for his grief, no meaning in any of the normal activities in which young men engage. Never a particularly gregarious person, Wilf became more solitary. His tears were shed privately; during the week his leisure hours were long seasons of private mourning in his dormitory lodgings. Wilf's older brother William and his wife, Isabel Hunter, pressed Wilf to spend the weekends with them. Nine months after the accident, these good people insisted that Wilf move in with them. Their flat was small, but they generously partitioned an already miniscule room to put up Wilfred. In that nine-month period, however, something else happened to Wilfred; something which gathered the shattered fragments of his life into a new pattern.

Wilf and Pat Urquhart with sons Robert and Andrew.

Brig. General Frank Frost and Mrs Frost.

Wilf and brother Robert Urquhart.

Chapter Two

A Glorious Conversion

In the Post Office Telegraph Department, a man named Willie Ross worked alongside Wilfred. Before Robert's accident, Willie had often talked to Wilf about Christianity, but his words fell on deaf ears. Wilf's interest was confined to the picture-house. He had absolutely no interest in spiritual things.

"Why not come down to the YMCA?" Willie had often invited Wilf, but with no success. Then, some time after the accident, Willie tried again. It took persistence, but one day, Wilf's response was different.

"Okay!" Wilf surprised Willie, indeed, surprised himself. All he knew of the YMCA was that it was a sports club where boys could play billiards and table-tennis. When he went to the YM that first night, however, he noticed the warmth of greeting he received.

"I noticed something else," Wilf acknowledged. "Everybody looked happy. My own life was adrift, and I could see these boys had something that I didn't have but wanted. Of course, at that time, I had no idea what that something was."

The first night at the YMCA Wilf met Joe Mackenzie, John Mackenzie, Derek Morrison, Derek Urquhart, and Secretary Tom MacDonald. Years later, Wilf was to discover that Willie Ross never attended the YMCA himself but Tom Macdonald was behind the persistent invitations, pushing Willie Ross hard to get Wilfred down to the Club.

"I enjoyed the evening," Wilf continued. "I was handed over to Duncan Urquhart and we played darts and billiards. Then we had tea and I noticed again how happy these people were. They have something, I thought to myself. I wondered what it could be."

At work, Willie Ross kept pushing Wilf to attend the Club. Gradually, the stricken boy's evenings were more often than not spent at the YM. He'd found friends, and the emptiness of his heart felt less acute. But he was still far from the peace that passes understanding, the peace that comes from God alone. One night, a crisis occurred. Wilfred remembers it well.

"My good friend Duncan invited me to come to a Bible class one night." It was a well-intended invitation and perhaps in the providence of the Almighty what happened needed to happen so things could be brought to a head. "I asked Duncan what a Bible Study was. He told me that the boys studied the Bible and learned more about God and about how He loves us." At Duncan's words, something snapped in Wilfred.

"God doesn't like me, and I hate God." The wounded lad almost screamed in his sudden rush of temper. "Don't ever talk to me again about God." With that, Wilf stalked out of the Club, leaving poor Duncan to wonder what he had said wrong.

Some weeks later, however, Wilfred came back, drawn once again by the contrast between his own inward emptiness and the obvious reality of the "something these guys had." Everyone was friendly and glad to see him, but nobody invited him to Bible studies again. (Secretary Tom MacDonald, who always tried to be "as wise as a serpent and as harmless as a dove" had instructed the other boys to keep silent and let God do His own work in Wilfred's heart).

"One night I went to the YM and found the place empty, or so I thought," Wilf recounted. "I played a game of billiards myself. That was no fun. Then I thought I heard voices in the front room. When I pushed the door it kind of flew open and I barged in - right into the middle of a Bible Study. Since I more or less landed in the middle of the room, I was too embarrassed to leave. I sat down on the nearest chair."

The speaker that night was Brigadier-General Frost. A

renowned Christian man, Brigadier-General Frost was also a superb Bible teacher. That night he spoke on prophetic Scriptures, lecturing for over ninety minutes. Having no prior knowledge of the subject, Wilf was bored and fidgety - until about ten minutes before the end.

"That's when Brigadier-General Frost began to detail the eternal destiny of those people outside of Christ." Wilf speaks reverendly of that night. "As the Word became more and more clear to me, two words impressed themselves so strongly in my heart that I almost thought they were from outside of my own mind. The two words were, 'That's you!' I knew that the graphic details the speaker used simply described my eternal destiny."

Brigadier-General Frost concluded the meeting by suggesting that anybody in the room who needed to should pray the simple prayer which he then verbalized. Wilf didn't pray. When tea was served after the meeting, Wilf realized something.

"My hands were trembling so violently, I couldn't hold my tea-cup." Shaking his head as he retells the story, Wilf continues. "I had to wrap both hands around the cup."

Deeply troubled in soul, Wilfred went home to his dormitory shared by six other young men. He didn't speak to anybody. Instead, he pulled the sheet right over his head and, in the darkness of the room, spoke quietly to God out of the depths of a Spirit-convicted heart. Not knowing much Scripture, but knowing that he was a sinner who needed to be saved, Wilf prayed the prayer Brigadier-General Frost had suggested.

"Whosoever shall call upon the Name of the Lord shall be saved," God's Word declares. Wilf didn't know that Bible promise then, but God did something wonderful. As Wilfred Urquhart cried out to the Lord Jesus in repentance and faith, a car on the other side of the river opposite Wilfred's room made a wide sweeping turn. The arc of the headlight's strong beam momentarily flooded the room with light, shining right through the white sheet which covered the praying boy's head.

"No sooner had I prayed, than this light came." Wilfred chuckled. "I knew right away what it was - other cars had done the same thing before. But coming when it did, the light brought a thought to me. I felt it so strongly that I almost want to say it was God's Word to my heart. I thought, 'The light of God's love is breaking into your heart and you are now saved.' Later, I would find many Bible statements which explicitly affirm the thought which gripped my heart at that moment. One thing I can say. I knew then that God had saved me. In all the years since, I have never lost that assurance."

From that day, Willie Ross no longer had to push Wilf to attend the Club. The next night, Wilfred was back at the YMCA. "First thing I did was tell the boys what had happened to me," he recalled. "Their faces were a picture when I told them. They were over the moon with joy."

Through faith in the Lord Jesus Christ, Wilfred Urquhart not only had the forgiveness of sins, and the assurance of eternal life - he also found himself brought into a spiritual fellowship as a member of "the church which is His body... ."(Ephesians 1:22,23) Wilfred had found the "something" which other young men in Inverness had found before him and, by God's wonderful grace, Wilf was going to have the privilege of seeing others also find.

Wilf's conversion was the start of a wonderful new life. His story will be resumed later. But what of this Inverness YMCA which God used to bring young Wilf Urquhart to inward peace and outward change? What of the young men there who "had something", that seemingly elusive something which Wilf Urquhart recognized and desired for himself? What of the Secretary, Tom MacDonald, and other dedicated workers who, surrendering all to the Lord, had chosen to pour them-selves out in selfless ministry to the young people, especially

the young men, of Inverness? These and other questions will
be at least partially answered in the following chapters which
attempt to record the flow of events forming the history of
Inverness YMCA.

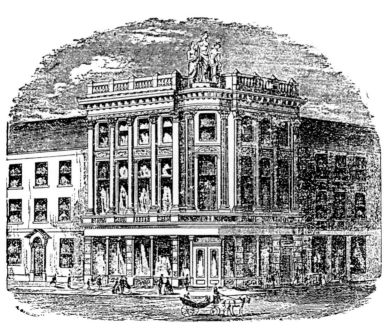

YMCA Buildings 1880.

YMCA Board of Management 1925.

Chapter Three
Inverness YMCA Beginnings

The first stirrings which gave birth to Inverness YMCA must remain shrouded in mystery since written records, if they ever existed, did not survive the years. Officially, the YMCA made its first public appearance through a notice in an 1859 Inverness Advertiser which read, "The object of this association is to further the interests of young men. By means of library, reading room, lectures, devotional meetings, Bible and other classes, the Association will strive to attain the object aimed at. Considerable expense will have to be incurred on fitting the rooms about to be occupied by the Association. The Committee therefore appeals to all interested in the religious and mental improvement of young men to help them in this good work. Subscriptions and donations of books will be thankfully received by the Treasurer, Mr. J. Fraser, Ironmonger, Inglis St; the Secretary; or any member of the Committee." (Inverness, May, 1859.)

Behind that first advertisement, however, lay the dedicated desires and determined commitment of five Christian townsmen. They were William Morrison, shipowner; J. Fraser, ironmonger; these two are certain. Perhaps the others were George Walker, Lumber yard owner; Alex Maclennan Grocer, Bridge St; and Wm. Corner, or James Barron, Editor. Quite clearly, these men (and likely their wives and friends) felt a compelling desire to reach young men in Inverness and district with the life-changing Gospel of their Lord and Saviour Jesus Christ.

Though scant information exists from formal records, the annals on high record the full story of how these five men responded to the burden they felt for the young men of their day. We can guess that their common concerns led them to concerted prayer, then to shared dreams, and from there to planned action. Through the one hundred and thirty-three year period which separates us from these intrepid souls, we can, with sanctified imagination, hear their bold entreaties to heaven in the early stages of their enterprise. We can believe that long hours were set aside to discuss the spiritual needs of country boys coming into the town for apprenticeship or other work. We can surmise that the burden these men carried extended beyond apprentices to large numbers of town and country boys surrounded with temptation and all to often uninstructed in the ways of the Most High.

Probably the original founders of Inverness YMCA were aware of places like Glasgow YMCA (the world's oldest YMCA, predating George Williams world-wide organization by twenty years) Founded by David Naismith on February 13, 1924 under the name of "The Young Men's Society for Religious Improvement", membership in Naismith's Clubs were for "young men, between the age of 14 and 35, of good moral character and professing no opinions subversive of evangelical principles. ... The Bible is considered as their rule and all political discussion is prohibited." (Taken from a letter written in 1837 by David Naismith to a friend.) A number of such associations came into existence through Naismith's efforts. When George Williams organized similar young men's groups, he introduced the principle of confining membership in his organization to young men of professed Christianity - though most YMCA's of today are very far removed from that principle.

David Naismith's Young Men's Associations, forerunners of William's YMCA's, offered an annual sermon for young men, library facilities, a literary institute, and evening educational classes. As well, there came into being an evangelistic mission for tract distribution and open air Gospel meetings.

Bible classes were also begun.

Although there was nothing like that in the Highlands of Scotland, there appears to have been a need and a hunger as the initial notice in the Inverness Advertiser enjoyed good response. Before year-end, the newspaper noted the establishment of a public reading room situated at 3 High Street - next door to premises which, within a decade, would be demolished to make room for the beautiful new YMCA building finished in 1869. But we get ahead of ourselves.

Inverness YMCA programme activities commenced with the reading room and a series of public lectures designed to strengthen Christian influence in the lives of the hearers. Local ministers supported the new Association by, among other things, presenting the public lectures. One, given on January 6, 1863, is typical. Its title? "The Church in Christ's Hands for Protection and Advancement to the Ultimate Consummation." If the subject appears heavy, at least the advertisement closed with the welcome words, "Admission Free."

Each Sabbath evening, after the local churches had completed their services of praise, young people and old made their way from their place of worship to the YMCA rooms. Was there a nationally-famous conference speaker retained by one of the Inverness churches that weekend? His Sabbath day ended with yet one more address to the YMCA. At other times, Inverness and district ministers capped their Lord's Day labours by preaching a word of exhortation to the Inverness Christians sitting together at the YMCA. Denominational differences laid aside, the fifty, seventy or a hundred plus representatives of protestant Christendom were a visual demonstration of the world-wide YMCA motto - "All One In Christ Jesus."

According to a YMCA Scottish National Council survey of 1895, Inverness YMCA ranks ninth earliest in date of beginning, sharing that position with Aberdeen which also commenced operations in 1859. Perhaps this shared position brought into being the mutual respect and support which has always marked the two Associations.

In 1863 the fourth annual report of the infant Inverness association announced a total membership of 49 and a financial deficit of 6 pounds sterling carried over from the previous year. Nevertheless, general satisfaction prevailed, as the deficit in the previous year had been 20 pounds. The prospect of continuing growth in the membership gave strong grounds for hope that future year-end balances would stay on the plus side of the ledger.

The earliest printed list of Association rules is dated 1875, when Inverness YMCA was seventeen years old. However, it is likely that these rules had prevailed since the Association's beginnings. The rules are as follows:

I.

That this Society be called "The Inverness Young Men's Christian Association."

II.

That the object of the Association be the improvement of the spiritual and mental condition of young men.

III.

That the means employed for the attainment of this object be the personal efforts of the Members of the Association, Devotional Meetings, Biblical Instruction and Literary Improvement, the Delivery of Lectures, the Diffusion of Christian Literature, a Library and Reading Room, and any other means in accordance with the Word of God.

IV.

That the affairs of the Association be conducted by the Office-bearers and a Committee of Management, who shall meet as often as necessary for the despatch of Business. Five to form a quorum. The Committee shall be elected annually by a majority of Members at a Meeting to be held for that purpose in the last week of December.

V.

That an Annual Meeting be held the first week of January at which a Report of the proceedings of the Association shall be read.

VI.

That Meetings be held in connection with the Association for the purpose of prayer, reading the Scriptures, mutual edification and encouragement, and for receiving information on all matters tending to promote the welfare of the Association; at which meetings any Member shall have the privilege of introducing his friends. That the Chairman of each Meeting be appointed by the Committee, and that all meetings shall begin and end with prayer.

VII.

That any person shall be eligible for Membership who gives evidence of his conversion to God; that he shall be proposed by a member of the Association at any of its Meetings, and elected by the Committee, after a satisfactory inquiry as to his suitability.

VIII.

That the Committee shall possess power to suspend or exclude any Member whose conduct is found, in their judgment, inconsistent with the Christian character.

IX.

That no charge shall be made for mere Membership; but Members of the Association shall be admitted to the privileges of the Library, Reading-Room, Lectures, and Classes, on the following terms:- Apprentices, 4 shillings Yearly, which may be paid Quarterly, Ordinary Members, 8 shillings and upwards. Honorary Members, 20 shillings.

X.

That persons not Members of the Association shall be admitted, on the same terms, to the privileges enjoyed by the Members, but the right of voting at all Meetings shall be confined to the Members; and that Young Men coming to town shall be admitted to the Reading-Room without fee for One Month.

Though the Inverness churches willingly cooperated with the YMCA, minor problems had been noted in 1863 when the increase of attendance at the Sunday afternoon Bible Class resulted in some churches becoming short of Sunday School teachers. How the problem was resolved is not known, but it seems the advantages offered to young Christians by the YMCA were recognized as outweighing these small difficulties. Along with the weekly Bible class, members participated in a keen ministry of tract distribution; and shared the benefits of a Reading Room which was becoming increasingly well-stocked with newspapers, periodicals, and otherwise hard to procure books. (The 1863 AGM report mentions thanks to George France, Esq., for the donation of 77 volumes).

Chapter Four

Reaching Out To 'Wicked Boys'

In that first ten year period of its history, Inverness YMCA was undergirded by a tremendous cross-section of public support. Not only the churches, but civic leaders offered at least token support to the new organization. In 1866 the seventh Annual General Meeting of the YMCA attracted an audience of between five and six hundred people including "many influential gentlemen and clergy". Shipowner Morrison occupied the chair and then-secretary Mr. Macleod of the Caledonian Bank read the reports. Eighteen new members were welcomed during the year being reported on; a surplus of over 8 pounds was carried forward in the general fund; and a donation of 100 pounds was received for the proposed new building. Also, a "Mutual Improvement Society" had been formed.

When one learns that in those days an admission fee was charged for entrance to the AGM, it becomes obvious that these hundreds of people attended because of a genuine desire to support the ministries embraced by the organisation.

An editorial paragraph fortuitously lying alongside the YMCA 1868 AGM report in the Inverness Advertiser acts as a window to show the context of work among youth in Inverness. Though quaint to the present-day reader, the article also shows the class of boys the YMCA hoped to attract, evangelize and elevate to a higher level of living. The subject of the article was Pauper's Funerals.

"A correspondent complains of the indecent manner in which pauper's funerals are conducted in this town - a hearse,

followed by two half-imbecile lads making up the whole
cortege. These lads, being the butt of wicked boys, are apt to
be hooted and yelled at in passing as they were on a recent
occasion, and the solemn ceremony was then turned into
ridicule. This, our correspondent says, he has witnessed more
than once; and, if the facts be as stated, we think that common
decency demands an instant amendment to the practice."

"Wicked boys." Ordinary lads without privilege of education or decent social status. Still, boys for whom Christ died.
The aim of the Association was to win souls and to this end,
the unchurched "wicked boys" of the street became as much
the focus of the YMCA programmes as more fortunate boys
from Christian homes or who were already linked to a
Christian church.

By 1869, the tenth anniversary of its inception, Inverness
YMCA had broken new ground in instituting several important outreach ministries. One was the Davis Square Evening
School, formed in 1867, "for the instruction of apprentices and
working lads in reading, writing and arithmetic as well as in
Scriptural Knowledge, in aid of which the Committee had to
acknowledge, without asking one penny, the receipt of more
money than paid its expenses,and especially a collection made
in the Free Church on Christmas by the Rev. D. Fraser of his
own good will."

The Davis Square evening school obviously met a pressing
need as over ninety young men, eager to learn, crowded the
classes which met three nights a week. The significance of this
practical ministry comes into focus when one remembers that,
at the time, education was still a privilege of the few. The
National Education Act did not come into effect until 1872 -
a full five years after Inverness YMCA initiated Davis Square
Evening Classes.

The 1868 Annual Report makes no reference to building
plans. Nonetheless, Invernessians reading the account of the

YMCA 1869 Annual General Meeting observed the following: "The Association's new building at the corner of High Street and Church Street is nearing completion. Fund-raising plans include a Bazaar (proposed by the Ladies). True friends of Inverness, at home and abroad, are expected to help. The building, which is conducive to the best interests of the community, is also architecturally an ornament to the town." At that time, four hundred of the required three thousand pounds had been contributed to the Building Fund.

At least one member of the clergy was caught in conflict between his desire that the YMCA should prosper and his reservations about some fund-raising techniques. Reporting on an address delivered by Rev. Mr. Robson, the Inverness Advertiser writer said, "He (Rev. Robson) hoped the grand bazaar would make large additions to Association funds. He would not express his individual opinion in reference to the bazaar, but one good feature in connection with them was that they brought into operation the agency of that marvellous little instrument the needle. He had no doubt if it was industriously applied in Inverness, it would stitch together a pretty large sum for the Association. (Applause). The young men depended upon the ladies and hoped by their aid to have the new building crowned with the finest ornament of all - freedom from debt. (Applause)."

Again, gaps in the record rob us of details about the outcomes of these fund-raising projects. What is known is that the new building was fully operative before the next AGM. Located acros the road from the old Town Hall, in the very centre of town, the YMCA Rooms became known as one of the architectural gems of Inverness. Topped by a uniquely beautiful triune statue of three female figures, standing nine feet tall, representing Faith, Hope, and Charity, the spacious and attractive building quickly became the hub of multiple programmes for and ministries of the YMCA members. (These figures now reside in a private museum in Orkney. It is hoped that they will be returned to Inverness where they were such a distinctive monument to three generations of Invernessians.) On weekdays, the rooms were open from 8:a.m until 10:p.m. Weeknights featured lectures from various speakers.

On the first Monday which introduced the lectures, the speaker was James Barron of the Inverness Courier who spoke on the subject "A Holiday Ramble." Since Mr. Barron, a great Christian and a great lover of God's Creation, later founded the Inverness Field Club, one can assume it was a lively and elucidating experience for the hearers.

On Tuesdays, a literacy class was conducted. Also, a teacher named William Snowie taught French for those interested in acquiring that language. A fragment of the value of these educational efforts is found in a letter read by the secretary to the AGM of 1871. "We have received communication," he advised. "From young men in distant lands who had attended that class and were now doing well."

On another evening, the Mutual Aid Society stimulated the minds of the lads through debate and discussion while painlessly implanting in them skills of logic, organization and public speech.

Other evenings were set aside for weekly prayer meetings; Bible studies; Open Air Evangelistic work (at the Exchange in front of the Town Hall); and tract distribution. In one sense, it was a day of small beginnings. But it is impossible to estimate how many young Christian men first learned how to speak up for Jesus Christ in the Open Air meetings. Sometimes the butt of human ridicule, sometimes the instrument of God's grace to seeking souls, these earnest young Christians confessed Christ in personal testimony and urgent entreaty for others to seek the Lord and His salvation.

So, leisure educational and spiritual activities formed the YMCA programme, with spiritual activities predominating. In those days, every activity was intended to bring young men off the streets and, ultimately, under the sound of the Gospel. As one general secretary expressed it (AGM,1869), "Above all, the aim of the Association is to win souls to Christ, and already it has begun to experience tokens of that blessing which at this time is being so richly poured out upon our native land."

Another Inverness YMCA leader of the period, Mr. Corner, wrote, "The principal ingredient in their fellowship is the love of Christ. This is good cement to build the house. ... (we must) continue to cultivate piety and prayer."

John Mackenzie, M.D., residing at Eileanach on Island Bank Road, was President of the Association in 1869. Concurrent with this and his onerous duties as medical doctor, this man was also Provost of the town. In those early days, perhaps it took men of substance to commence social and spiritual programmes to elevate the general welfare of their community. But the men God used to start and maintain the YMCA were also men of spiritual substance. Their names appear in connection with their individual church societies; with interdenominational foreign mission societies; and with local united evangelistic efforts springing from the grand ecumenicity of different denominations seeking to honour the Lordship of Jesus Christ. One such united campaign linked Inverness and the Highlands with the work of grace God was doing elsewhere in Britain through Dwight L. Moody and Ira Sankey. Some details of this event are recorded in the "Report for 1874", the earliest surviving record available produced by the Association itself. For the reader's interest, this report is reproduced in its entirety in the next chapter.

SPECIAL VISIT

of the

REV. DR.

JOHN WESLEY WHITE

International Evangelist

formerly of Florida, now of Cumnor, Oxford

with DR. WHITE'S THREE SONS, who make a unique trio

(left to right)

Wesley — *Alto*

Paul — *Soprano*

Billy — *Tenor*

Y.M.C.A. HALL, Bank Street, Inverness

Tuesday Aug. 30 to Sunday Sept. 11th

(Inclusive)   ALL MEETINGS AT 8 p.m.

No meetings on Saturdays

SUNDAY AFTER=CHURCH RALLY

EMPIRE THEATRE, ACADEMY STREET, 8 p.m.

Don't miss these outstanding meetings—
YOU are welcome

PHILLIPS · PRINTER · EASTBOURNE

Handbill — John Wesley White.

Chapter Five

Report for 1874

Office-Bearers

Honorary President:	H. M. Matheson, Esq., London.
President:	John Mackenzie, Esq. of Eileanach,
Vice-President:	Wm. Morrison, Esq.
Treasurer:	Alexander Maclennan
Secretary:	William Corner

Committee

James Fraser; Arthur Robertson; William Dingwall; A. Watt; William MacGregor; Duncan Mackintosh; Arthur Robertson; John MacDonald; M. G. Mackenzie; Alexander Maclennan; James Barron;

Librarian;	J. Dunoon
Secretary of Tract Society;	John Burnside

The Committee has to record with deep thankfulness the blessing given to the Association during the past year. It has, with other Christian institutions throughout the country, shared in a renewed life and in successful labours. Its special aim has been the ingathering of young men to Jesus Christ, and this aim has, by the divine blessing, been in measure accomplished. It is felt that youth is the time for decision, and that without conversion no permanent good will be done to the young men who come within the influence of the Association. In aiming high, there is more likelihood of higher attainments, and while intellectual culture has not been neglected, the special feature of the year has been Evangelistic work.

In the beginning of 1874, attention was directed to Edinburgh, where there was an extensive work of grace going on, and the desire was very general that the movement should spread over the land. The annual week of prayer in January was, under these circumstances, held with more than usual interest, the evening meetings in the Union Street church being continued for three weeks, while a daily meeting for prayer at noon was begun in the Association Hall simultaneously with the evening meeting, and continued till September.

In March it was agreed to hold in concert with other towns a week of special services for young men. To make the meetings more successful,it was resolved to invite a deputation of the Edinburgh young men to assist, and the Secretary went to that city to press the claims on the committee there. Messrs. Stuart and Ritchie were sent, and the meetings began in the Hall on the 24th March with a large attendance. The Word was with power, and several waited at the close as enquirers. For three evenings the deputation remained, the interest deepening and numbers being awakened. For three weeks the meetings continued night after night, the ministers and young men freely taking part. At the close of each meeting numbers usually waited for conversion, and every room in the building was found occupied by enquirers who were pointed more clearly to the Cross, or by Christians pleading on their behalf. The series was brought to a close on the 10th by a Social Meeting, which crowded the Lower Hall, at which short addresses were given, and the Chairman and the Rev. George Robson gave a brief review of the meetings and of their results. Young men who are now members of churches in town were awakened at that time; and one young man, John Macaulay, from Sutherlandshire, who then found peace, has now, it is believed, joined the Church above. He was clerk in a solicitor's office, and from his robust form and healthy appearance, there seemed every prospect of his enjoying long life. He was, however, seized with illness early in December, and on the 18th of that month he died, aged 22.

In August, 1873, Messrs. Moody and Sankey, then labouring in Newcastle, were invited by the Association to Inverness. In December of that year a deputation of Ministers waited on them in Edinburgh, and obtained their promise to come.

An Evangelistic Committee, composed of members of various churches, was then formed to make arrangements, and on the 7th of July the Evangelists began their long expected services in Inverness. The usual daily order of the services was a Prayer Meeting in the Music Hall at noon; a Bible Reading in the Free High or Union Street Church at 3; a Gospel Meeting in the Free High Church at 8; and a meeting for men in the Congregational Church at 9. In addition to these, open air meetings were occasionally held on the Castle Hill, or in the New Park, at which immense numbers congregated. The labours of the Evangelists were prodigious, and much impression was made. Moody's great tact and power were nowhere seen to greater advantage than in the men's meetings. His clear teaching and direct way of dealing with souls gave many useful lessons to those who sought to be soul gatherers. On the 27th of August Moody held his "farewell convention for Scotland" in the West Church, Inverness. There was a large gathering of strangers, and it is supposed that over 150 ministers of different denominations were present. They came from Orkney, Caithness, Sutherland, Lewis, Skye, and the neighbouring counties, while Aberdeen, Glasgow, Edinburgh, London, and other places sent representatives. Moody occupied the chair during the whole service which lasted from 10 a.m. to 4 p.m. the different subjects were opened by the leading men of the country, and ministers and others took part in the conversation. In the evening an Evangelistic meeting was held in the same place, which was literally crammed. Moody again presided, and several addresses were given. The 27th of August is a day much to be remembered by the hundreds who were gathered together, and the blessing which was then given must have had a powerful influence over the Highlands.

Another series of meetings for young men was held in the rooms in November, which, although not so largely attended as the previous series, nor with such apparent results, were yet felt to be a source of much good. A week of mixed meetings followed (men and women) which were well attended.

Membership

During the year 20 members were admitted, two died and two left for other places, leaving the number on the roll 88. The Associates, or the members of the different classes, number 85, making a total of 165 in connection with the Association. The Committee record with regret the death of the Rev. Wm. Milne, who became a member in 1871. He took a warm interest in the affairs of the Association, and had he been left in health would have been of great service. For a considerable time before his death he was laid aside, and in January 1874 was called home. The other member who died was Donald McGregor, printer, who joined the Association in 1873. Although young in years he took an active interest in all the work of the Association. Often would he tell what great things the Lord had done for him, and the memory of his slight form, earnest voice, and stirring words seems to linger round these rooms which to him had proved a place of blessing. For some months before his death he was confined to the house, and latterly was compelled to sit night and day in an arm chair. Through all the weary weeks of suffering not a murmur escaped his lips. His was a triumphant faith which expressed itself not in sighs and groans, but in calm trust and cheerful confidence. It was a real pleasure to sit beside that chair, and holding his clammy hands, to hear him speak of his Beloved, and of the goodness of the Lord. The young men delighted to nurse him by turn, and the long nights would be shortened by fervent prayer and joyful songs of praise in which the Association was often remembered.

This, then, was the report given to the annual meeting of 1874. In moving the adoption of the report, Rev. J. Howard acknowledged that he would never forget some of the hallowed scenes he had witnessed in these rooms, and the services in which he was privileged to take part.

Another speaker referred to the leading part which the Association took in Messrs. Moody and Sankey's visit, which visit had been felt as an impulse for good all over the Highlands. (Some eighty years later Inverness YMCA members were once again involved in a major evangelistic campaign. The young men conducted an extended series of all-night prayer meetings in preparation for the one-day visit of Dr. Billy Graham to Inverness. Dr. Graham preached in Bught Park to 20,000 people with many coming forward in response to the Gospel invitation. In cooperation with the Christian Business Men's Committee, Inverness YMCA played a prominent part in this event.)

In 1874, yet another speaker, Mr. Adam Humberston, likened the operations of grace to the operations of agriculture. He mentioned that some weeks ago he travelled by train with some men of the Naval Reserve who were returning home after completing their drill in Inverness. One of them was reading a religious book, and on enquiry Mr. Adam found that the Naval man had been awakened through the efforts of the Young Men's Christian Association since coming to Inverness, and that now he was resolved to lead a new and better life.

Dr. George Mackenzie, Church Street, pointed out the field

for the operations of such a society. The whole of the North of
Scotland sent in their young men to Inverness, and it was the
work of the Association to care for their wants, both spiritual
and temporal.

The Rev. Mr. MacDonald, Nairn, spoke of the thoroughness
needed by Christians and a Christian Association. There was
danger in a Society outstepping its true work, but from the
Report read, this could not be said of the Inverness Association. His remarks were followed by an acknowledgement from
Mr. A. Maclennan, Inverness, who spoke of the good which
he had derived from the Association and advocated its extension and continued effort.

Such, then, was the gracious work of God in Inverness
YMCA from its inception in 1859 until 1875. Elsewhere in the
world, momentous events unfolded. In 1859, Darwin published his Origin of Species by Means of Natural Selection;
John Stuart Mill, his essay On Liberty; and Karl Marx, exiled
in London, published his Critique of Political Economy.
These men and their works would change the face of British
society, indeed that of the civilized world.

In America, Abraham Lincoln was elected President on
November 6, 1860. Keeping his promise to abolish slavery, he
paid for that with his life only five years later when John
Wilkes Booth shot him to death.

In those years, Florence Nightingale fired the imagination of
every little British girl by her heroic nursing exploits in the
Crimean War, reported widely in the daily Press. A little later,
one reads of a canal being opened at Suez (1869). And, a new
machine, the typewriter, was introduced on the market.

Amongst the changes of the period was one which occurred
in Rome on July 18, 1870. The Vatican General Council
passed, by an overwhelming majority, (which suggests a more
enlightened minority) the dogma Pastor Aeternus which
declares that the Pope, when he speaks as "Shepherd and

Teacher of all Christians," enjoys infallibility in defining doctrine on faith and morals, his doctrines being "unalterable in themselves and not by virtue of the assent of the church..."

In Scotland, the Bible still ruled as the only infallible and trustworthy inspired Word of God. The Bible, not the word of any man, ruled in the Inverness YMCA rooms. There, under the watchful care of Faith Hope and Charity, God's gracious blessings continued to influence the lives of young men through the various programmes, the details of which follow.

Members in the late 1950's.

1957 — Derek Morrison, Duncan Quinn, Wesley White, Mrs White, Dr Wesley White, Billy White, George Henderson, John Macpherson, Rev. John McBeth, Alick Archibald.

Chapter Six

Building Up - Reaching Out

In February of 1875, the Secretary of Inverness YMCA communicated that the ordinary Weekly meetings of the Association were being conducted in a similar way to those of previous years and on the same evenings. Those present at the AGM heard the following summary of each segment of the work.

The Fellowship Meeting, on Wednesday night, has had occasional interruption from special services, which may account somewhat for its attendance not being so large as desirable. The subjects of study were taken from Romans and Hebrews and were very profitable.

The Prayer Meeting has been held during the year on Friday evenings. The attendance has fluctuated considerably, but prayer has not ceased to be offered for much spiritual blessing.

The Bible Conversational Class was held every Thursday. In the summer season a prize book, presented by a former classfellow was competed for by an essay on John 14:6. The winner was Mr. Donald Ross, and the other competitors also received books, the essays being well expressed, and showing a fair understanding of the subject.

The Bible Class is held, as usual, every Sabbath afternoon at five o'clock. Since Mr. Campbell left for Edinburgh, Mr. Watt has been sole teacher, and considerable interest has been taken in the subjects of study.

The Mutual Improvement Society has continued to meet on Tuesday evenings during the winter months. The session is described by the Secretary as a most brilliant one. The number on the roll is about 60. Essays have been given on various

interesting subjects, the discussion of which displayed no
small amount of literary ability. A prominent feature in the
syllabus has been a course of lectures, kindly given by Mr.
Wallace of the High School, on geology, archaeology, and
English literature. These lectures have been held in the
Rooms, with free admission and good attendance, numbers of
young men not belonging to the Association being present.

In addition to the Annual Meeting and Christmas Breakfast,
five free Social Meetings for young men were given during the
year. Two of these were for the men of the Naval Reserve who,
on each occasion, filled the lower hall; the other meetings were
for the young men of the town of whom the attendance
averaged 100. The social element proves a great attraction and
without it, in many instances, the class desired cannot be
drawn together. Good has been done at those meetings, and the
various friends who contributed to their success, financially
and otherwise, are warmly thanked.

Prominent in the department of Evangelistic Work is the
Sabbath evening meeting which has been held during the year
in the Hall from 8 to 9 o'clock. The attendance averaged about
200, composed mostly of young people. The service is chiefly
prayer and praise, with a short, pointed address by some of the
ministers or members of the Association; and a good word has
often been spoken by strangers during the summer months.
This meeting has been a source of much blessing and has
proved very helpful in bringing young men to the Association.

On the 16th, 19th, and 20th June, 1875, Messrs. Bigland,
White, and Ramsay, three young men from Liverpool, con-
ducted evangelistic services in the open air and in the Hall, and
from the 1st to the 10th July similar services were held nightly,
the speakers being the Rev. John Morgan of London; Mr. R.
MacDougall, Liverpool; Mr. Bevers, Hull; Rev. Mr. Morrison,
Urquhart; Rev. Mr. Martin, Elgin; and several others - Mr.
Martin having to bear a large share of the work during the

Wool Market week. There was a large attendance at each meeting - principally of working men - and some professed to have received good.

During the summer months services were occasionally held in the country by some of the members. By invitation of Mr. Ogilvy of Corrimony, Drumnadrochit, meetings were conducted in the schoolhouse there every Sabbath from 8th Aug. to 7th Nov. at which, in addition to the English, a Gaelic address was occasionally given for the benefit of the older people. These meetings have been continued from November to the present time, with growing interest, by Mr. Campbell, farmer, Corrimony; and as the district is eight miles from church, the advantage of such a meeting will be apparent. Mr. Ogilvy has become an honorary member of the Association, and in many ways has shown his interest in the young men. A week of prayer for the work of the Association was observed in October and nightly meetings were held in the Rooms, with a good attendance.

The operations of The Scripture Reading And Tract Distribution Society continues to grow. From 1800 to 1900 "Monthy Visitors" have been distributed monthly in thirty-six districts in town and neighbouring villages - making a total of 22,100 "Monthly Visitors" left in the houses during the year. (The "Monthly Visitor" was a Gospel pamphlet distributed to homes and individuals on a regular monthly basis.)

Besides these, many thousands of Gaelic and English tracts have been scattered through town and country, the supplies having been ordered from the Religious Tract Society and Stirling Tract Society. At the close of the year there is a balance of 5 pence in hand; and as the annual payment of 17/6 (seven pounds, seventeen shillings, and sixpence) from the Association is insufficient to meet the growing expenses, friends will do well to remember this important department of work.

The Reading-room continues to be supplied with the local, and some of the leading, papers and periodicals. The Library has much need of renovation, many of the books being old and much perused. Good theological books for reference, and other standard works, are much required,and any spare volumes will be most thankfully received by the Librarian.

Lectures were delivered during the year by the Rev. A. White, of St. George's, Edinburgh, on Dante's "Purgatorio" and by the Rev. Dr. Donald Fraser, of London, on "Religion and Art." Both lectures were well attended, and the proceeds make a considerable addition to the income of the Association. (In 1875, the income from lecture admission fees was over 45 pounds, while expenses totalled 10 pounds. The profit, 35 pounds, added up to over 10% of the YM's entire income for the year.)

On the 16th of April a juvenile musical demonstration, conducted by Mr. Roddie, in aid of the Association, was held in the Music Hall, which was much appreciated. To all these gentlemen for their gratuitous services, and to the many helpers during the year, hearty thanks are given.

Further notes on the fifth National Conference of delegates from Associations in Scotland referred to the ongoing effects of the previous year's revival; and the Treasurer's Report indicated significantly increased income, expenditures, and the happy fact of a balance in hand of over 40 pounds. The debt on the building still amounted to just under 3,000 pounds. The day was looked forward to when the debt would be cleared thus allowing the YMCA to have its Rooms entirely devoted to the purposes of the Association·

The 1875 Annual Report ends with a paragraph entitled Conclusion, which reads:

A brief outline has been given of the various agencies at work, but in the history of such an institution, the unrecorded parts are often the best. There is the mutual strengthening, the individual effort, and the savour of a Christian life, which is more powerful than many precepts. In addition to combined effort, it would be well if each member would accept the Harlan Page Covenant - "Resolved that by Divine grace I will act as though there were no one else to act, waiting not for others." (Source of the Harlan Page Covenant is not cited.)

About the end of the year Mr. John Munro, who has been connected with the Association for some years, was led to give up business so that he might be able to devote himself more fully to Christian work. It was considered that there would be a great advantage in securing his services for the Association, and after much prayer he was, in January 1876, engaged as Assistant Secretary. Already the meetings show signs of renewed interest, and young men are being looked up who were before allowed to drop out of acquaintance. Ministers and friends would do well to send a letter of introduction with young men from the country to the Secretary or Assistant Secretary, and every attention will be paid to them.

Such, then, was the substance and spirit of the Inverness YMCA as a sixteen year old organisation. Innovative programmes to attract youth were combined with earnest personal efforts to win these youth for Jesus Christ. The Club (as it was known to many) was itself in a kind of adolescent stage - holding fast to the faithful Word, yet willing to risk new approaches to young people outside the pale. By 1883, when the membership had risen to 127, three members had already left the Club to labour as colporteurs in Ireland - no easy mission field in those days. Two other members were ministry students. They were the first, or among the first, of a long line of young men whom God called to full-time ministry from the ranks of Inverness YMCA membership.

Allenby Bridge over the Jordon.

The Wailing Wall.

The Star of Bethlehem.

Chapter Seven

"The Best Of All Twenty-Nine Years"

The newspaper reports of Annual General Meetings for the years between 1875 and 1883 offer tantalizing clues about the vibrant growth of YMCA outreach ministries.

As noted above, 1876 saw the engagement of a full-time paid secretary, a man named John Munro. Mr. Munro, who left secular employment because he felt called of God to Christian service, spoke Gaelic as well as English, an important capability in the Highlands of those day. However, for reasons unrecorded, he withdrew from the position six months after starting.

In 1877 Inverness YMCA conducted special work in the areas of visiting the sick; holding branch Bible classes during winter in the Merkinch and Central schools; organising social specials for men of the Naval Reserve; setting up special meetings for navvies employed at the Culduthel Water Works project; arranging meetings at Fort George for the Militia there and at Muir of Ord for the Highland Light Infantry Militia. As well, 2,000 tracts were distributed each month.

Another departure point involved the members of Inverness YMCA in a survey of four public houses where members stood outside and counted the number of people entering the premises. In approximately one four hour period, 2128 townsmen made use of the drinking establishments under survey. The survey was repeated the following week with even larger numbers being observed. The specific reasons for the survey are not now known, but clearly the YMCA was willing to find out for itself the full nature of its ministry concerns.

In 1878 a great storm on New Year's Eve (the infamous Hogmanay of annual Highland excess) kept many foreign ships in Inverness Harbour. A large group of sailors (representing many languages) took in the New Year at a social put on by the YMCA. Efforts were made that night to minister the Word and host the individuals in their own language.

The following year, 1879, a Mission work was undertaken in Davis Square where Sabbath School enrolled fifty children who were taught the Scriptures by ten teachers. Other evangelistic meetings were also conducted there for the residents of the area.

An interesting aside to the regular work of the Club occurred in February of 1882, when Britain's beloved Queen Victoria was shot at while on her way to Balmoral. (The fateful event happened in England). Although the would-be assassin fired from close range, the revolver bullet missed the Queen, and the man was quickly overpowered. At the Inverness YMCA Annual General Meeting, it was agreed to send a telegram to Her Majesty. The telegram read:

From YMCA, Inverness
To Home Secretary, House of Commons, London.
The Chairman and members in our meeting assembled desire to express their devout thankfulness to God for the providential escape of their beloved Sovereign and Queen.

That same year had seen the acquisition of a full-time paid general secretary, a man named Mr. Lapslay. Though he only remained two years, during his tenure the records show the work extending its Mission services to other town districts, most notably Shore St. There, four meetings were held each week in a mission hall which later became an independent Mission under the auspices of Mr. George Walker, timber merchant. Mr. Walker also served on the YMCA committee and, for many years, existing records show his name connected with the Association.

Ships coming into harbour were also "tracted" by members reaching out to sailors from many foreign shores.

Perhaps the fact that Mr. Lapslay was free to conduct a personal visitation programme to all the young men of the YMCA helped these young men to maintain their enthusiasm and spiritual commitment to ministries which, though honouring to God and frequently blessed, were not easy or not invariably well received.

In 1883, the year the three members left for mission work in Ireland, YMCA front line mission work continued in Inverness. It appears that, until this time, The Scripture Reading and Tract Distribution Society had existed as a separate organisation working with the YMCA. Details are obscure as to its beginnings in the town, but it is a matter of record that Scripture Reading and Tract Distribution Society members worked under the auspices of Inverness YMCA almost since the Club was formed. In 1884, The Scripture Reading and Tract Distribution Society formally merged into the Association, becoming an integral part of the YMCA. At that time, twenty members undertook a systematic tract distribution through the town, with all churches being encouraged to participate. As well, the Sunday Bible Study Class, taught by Mr. James Barron of Inverness Courier, was well attended.

YMCA's had also been started in Dingwall and Tain by this time, and delegates from these associations attended the Inverness Annual General Meetings. By 1886, Invergordon, Golspie and Grantown also sent delegates. Although these satellite associations did not survive the years, their incorporation reveals the scope and energy of YMCA outreach.

That year, a snippet of history was recorded in the Chairman's opening comments. He, Mr. William Morrison, "was present at the formation of the Association 27 years ago, when only 6 members met in a room and had a consultation in reference to the inauguration of the work." Just that much information. No names or details. But at least the brief comment suggests that if Mr. Morrison's co-founders were as faithful as he, the Inverness YMCA was built on a solid foundation.

During the previous twelve months, four members left to prepare for missionary work or church ministry; 2400 tracts were being distributed monthly; and classes in English and Latin were being taught by a Mr. Kerr.

Space does not permit discussion of other organisations and societies set up to further Gospel outreach in the town. Nor can we discuss various church societies which developed in this period. Sufficient to say that a climate of evangelical zeal marked most of the churches and directed the lives of many individuals. The men who ran Inverness YMCA were also inextricably involved in their own churches and other mission societies. Through their efforts, world-renowned mission leaders were to find their way to Inverness to fan the flames of missionary zeal and encourage greater evangelical activity. For example, a note in Inverness Advertiser intimated the visit of J. Hudson Taylor for Sunday/Monday meetings on the subject, "The Gospel For the World." These meetings, held under the auspices of the United Evangelistic Committee, were advertised over the signature of William Corner, YMCA secretary. Mr. Corner may have been one of the founders of Inverness YMCA. He was certainly actively involved for many years.

The marked success of the entire YMCA activities in the Inverness of 1888 moved the chairman to describe it as "the best of all 29 years." A record number of members had been added; fruit from the Open Air ministry was noted; more that 32,600 tracts had been distributed; and the year finished with a financial balance in hand of over ten pounds. The number present at the AGM is not recorded, but the admission fee of one shilling must have helped them maintain their good fiscal balance. Perhaps they felt they had too much income - admission to the next year's AGM was only sixpence!

Interesting and creative efforts were made to reach and evangelize specific people groups within the larger population. For instance, in 1890, a social meeting for tailors (the trade, not the name) resulted in the formation of a society called The Tailor's Total Abstinence Society. In another YMCA creative effort, readers (young woman as well as young men) went to the places of employment and read the Scriptures to tailors as they worked.

The previous year, cottage meetings had been revived in outlying districts of the town. At Dunain, a Band of Hope had been formed in connection with the Dunain Mission. The Dunain Mission, run by Inverness YMCA, first met in property owned by Inverness District Asylum; later, land was gifted from Mr. Baillie on the nominal annual rent of one shilling sterling. The YMCA built the Mission Hall for the sum of 198 pounds.

Gaelic and English Gospel services were conducted. And Mr. Roger, the National YMCA evangelist for Scotland had visited along with Mr. Henderson-Smith the travelling secretary.

Notes dated February 18, 1890, again refer to Mr. Morrison's part as founder of the Inverness YMCA, but this time as "one of five who met on the first occasion." The Young Women's Christian Association Annual General Meeting of that year named Mrs. Morrison as treasurer of that organization, making it evident that Mr. Morrison's evident love and concern for the souls of youth was shared by his wife. "Heirs together of the grace of life" (1 Peter 3:7) they were also "companions in labour, and fellow-soldiers" (Philippians 2:25) - a commendable example for all married couples.

Delegates from Elgin attended the 1893 AGM, to hear the secretary report that no less than 44,000 tracts had been distributed that year. Dunain Mission meetings were well attended and welcomed by the local people as they had difficulty getting to church. Not only was it before the day of the motor car, but road systems were limited and subject to restrictions by weather. By bringing these services to the community, the YMCA was expediting worship and Gospel outreach beyond the reach of town churches. These Dunain Mission meetings were to continue for another sixty years until the encroachment of suburban Inverness and the establishment of local churches in the district rendered Dunain Mission ministry unnecessary.

The 1895 AGM reported the death of William Morrison, President of the Association from its founding in 1859. Delegates from Beauly, and Portmahomack joined those from other YMCA's. There was a change of secretary and other committee officers and a Mr. Stewart of Dundee left Christian work in America (where he was associated with D. L. Moody) to become permanent secretary of Inverness YMCA.

With the passing of Mr. William Morrison, an era ended. Yet, the Scriptural bedrock of the work he and his fellow-founders established ensured that the work survived the workmen. The dedication of Mr. Morrison and his partners was most clearly focussed in the establishment of Inverness YMCA. But, ultimately, Inverness YMCA was (and is) God's work, not theirs. To God alone would these pioneers ascribe thankful praise for all that was accomplished through them.

Generations of town youth owe a great debt of gratitude to the Inverness YMCA founding fathers who poured themselves out in ministry. Their wholehearted example set the tone for future decades of Inverness YMCA leaders who have striven to maintain the Christ-centred, Bible-based, quality of the Association's activities.

Chapter Eight

World War One

Inevitably, after William Morrison's demise, the next few years were marked by the deaths of the other pioneer leaders of YMCA work in Inverness. The Annual General Meeting of 1900 noted the passing of William Dingwall "one of the YMCA's oldest and most energetic members." The following year, tribute was paid to the late George Walker, "a member for over thirty years."

However, though God was burying His workmen, God was also continuing His work through others. New ideas kept forming themselves into programmes which extended the borders of YMCA influence. One such effort was an ambulance class from St. Andrew's Ambulance which, in 1897 offered proficiency certificates to successful candidates.

New names also appear among the list of leaders, names which have been written on the annals of Inverness commercial history. Mr. Melven, Bookseller, was on the 1900 committee. He may have been a member of the YMCA prior to this date; he may even have served on some sub-committee without his name appearing in the meagre records which remain. Providentially, his vast commitment to Christian work is recorded elsewhere. From the years 1896 to 1902, Mr. Melven prepared and published a monthly magazine entitled The Northern Evangelist. Volume One (twelve bound issues for the year 1896) is the only remnant known to survive and can be found in Inverness Public Library. The Northern Evangelist was an excellent magazine containing sermons from Dr. John Macdonald "The Apostle of the North" and other past and contemporary preachers. Also, children's stories and novel conversational Bible studies in the Scottish vernacular made the publication highly readable and full of spiritual food.

In 1902, the name of another well-known Inverness shop-keeper enters the records of Inverness YMCA. Mr. Asher the baker was a member of that year's Committee.

It appears that these and other Elisha-like men inherited the mantle of their Elijahs. The programmes continued to prosper; but the building debt was slow in reducing. In 1881, 2945 pounds was owed. By 1903 the debt had only dropped by 445 pounds. From that date until the 1930's no further mention is made of debt-reduction, though progress was no doubt made as the 1935 financial statement shows only one bond against the property in the very manageable amount of 1700 pounds. Records of a national survey done by the Scottish National Council of YMCA's in 1924-25 show the sum of 1700 pounds against Inverness YMCA, so obviously there had been good debt reduction sometime before 1924 and no reduction since.

The Inverness Advertiser, which is the major source of information about YMCA activities from the years 1859 to 1935 does not contain much information about Inverness YMCA programme activities from 1902 on. A few box advertisements, brief notices, sketchy abbreviated reports, allow us to glimpse the highlights of the next thirty years. Nor is it always clear which were YMCA sponsored activities and which were simply hall rentals. A case in point involves a meeting of 1909 when the Literary Society advertised a meeting in the YMCA rooms. Three political speakers were featured, one representing the Conservative party, a second the Liberal party, and a third the Labour party. (This kind of meeting certainly appears to be a departure from the original rule of Naismith's in his organisation, which original rule was carried over to the "All One in Christ" spirit of the YMCA.)

An athletic club was also started and reported on in the 1909 AGM. "It is hard to get the athletic club lads interested in spiritual things," the report read. Two disadvantages were noted. No billiard room. And, no card room. Lively discussion ensued around the question, "Can we have these and still keep the distinctive character of the Association?" This was a question which would always confront the YMCA leadership. Anxious not to offend established churches, nor to promote anything which may cause spiritual harm, the leadership also had to find ways and means to bring lads off the streets and out of the dark corners of the town into the YMCA and ultimately under the sound of the life-changing Gospel. The question was not settled that evening. Instead, renewed efforts were directed towards encouraging each present member to reach others and persuade them to come to the Club.

On March 1, 1910, The YMCA Mutual Improvement Society advertised a paper by Rev. John Reid, M.A. entitled "Interest and Power of Personality." Later the same month, the newly-formed YMCA Male Voice Choir presented a Sacred Concert, tickets sixpence each.

In March, 1913 and again in August, 1914, speaker at the Sabbath Evening service was John A. Mackay of Princeton Theological Seminary. An Inverness son, this student was to become a world Christian. After visiting South America John A. Mackay had a vision that, through education, God planned to do a mighty work in that spiritually oppressed country. In response to that vision, John went to Madrid for a year to acquire Spanish; after which he founded the Free Church of Scotland College in Peru. Some years later, God called John to Monte Video, Urugay where he became General Secretary of an existing YMCA, working among students. Later, John served as President of Princeton Theological Seminary.

During the first two decades of the 20th century in Inverness, other spiritually valuable activities were also taking place. In December, 1914, Gypsy Smith conducted a meeting in the Catch My Pal Hall at the bottom of Academy Street. The title of Gypsy Smith's talk was, "My Life from Gypsy Tent to Gospel Platform." The sponsoring organisation, Catch My Pal, was a Temperance Youth movement started by Mr. Anderson, Baker. His sons continued his bakery and his zealous work for God. The Anderson family have remained faithful supporters of Inverness YMCA.

During the years of the Great War (1914-1918) the complete facilities of the YMCA were utilized by the government for use of Her Majesty's troops. Since the soul-winning efforts of the Association swung back into action immediately after the end of the war, it is likely that meetings continued during the war years, probably in a local church or hall. No records or public notices can be found. It is known, however, that the YMCA facilities were used to house and feed the troops and that local women worked the canteens to look after the servicemen. These circumstances were repeated during the Second World War, and a description of the latter in all probability also describes the essentials of what happened in the Great War. YMCA activities between 1939 and 1945 were witnessed by Mrs. Jenny Martin, a sister to the late John Macpherson, Inverness Coal Merchant and, for many years, a local YMCA leader. (Mr. Macpherson was also in charge of the Soldier's and Sailor's Home located alongside the Playhouse Theatre at the junction of Academy and Inglis streets. A colourful character, Mr. Macpherson was a stereotype of the typical Highland gentry. He became President of the Inverness YMCA in 1968.)

"During the War, the women who ran the canteen and dormitories attempted to make it a home away from home," Mrs. Martin recalled. "Volunteer families often had troops in their homes where they could relax for their few brief days of leave. There were many Canadians, in fact servicemen from all over the globe and from a variety of regiments. We held a garden fete once a year to raise funds for helping the work among the troops. Also, John held a Sunday worship service."

We may assume that the Great War was similar in that Inverness YMCA volunteers went beyond material help to influence for the Lord those troops who came under their care. A statistical report of the Soldiers' and Sailors' Tea Room shows that in one week 3591 individuals were served. This gives some idea, not only of the work load but also of the field of missionary opportunity God gave these volunteer workers in the dark days of the war.

Perhaps the War contributed to what appears to have been an assault on the traditional Scottish Sabbath-keeping. On January 1, 1918, Inverness YMCA representatives were present at a large Public Meeting in the Free North Church to discuss the problem of the town magistrates granting a licence for a Sunday concert in the Music Hall. At the meeting, Mr. Corner, a retired banker and long-time executive member of the YMCA, spoke. "Mr. Macleod said his friends in the Management committee of the YMCA took their stand some time ago on the question of Sunday concerts. They (the YMCA) were offered the proceeds of the concert but refused point blank to have anything to do with it."

The above record also suggests that during the Great War a management committee had been active in preserving YMCA interests. The spiritual tone of their convictions is evident.

In 1919, a number of YMCA advertisements indicate that programmes were beginning to roll once more. In September the opening meeting of YMCA Boy's Club beckoned lads aged 12-18 to come to the Club at Raining House. (Presumably, the Forces' use of the YMCA rooms was not yet over.) The next month The Mutual Improvement Society welcomed former members and non-members to a re-starting programme.

By February, 1920, the YMCA once again occupied Castle Street rooms. It advertised a full programme as follows:

Sunday   3:30: Meeting for working lads.
Sunday   7:50. Men's Social Hour.
Thursday 7:30. Bible Meeting
Rooms open weekdays 10:a.m. to 10:p.m. Two first class billiard tables. The Gymnasium, Ardross St. For Men, Mon, Wed, Fri, 7:30. For Women, Tues. and Thurs.
Members Now being enrolled. Adult subscription, 5 shillings.

In time, advertisements for YMCA Literary Society, evening open air services at the Town Exchange, and the Male Voice Choir rounded out the Club programme activities.

In October, 1922, the High Parish Church and United Free High Church combined to present a three day mission with no less eminent a speaker than F. B. Meyer. The next month, well-know Scottish evangelists Jock Troup and Somerville Smith held a Gospel campaign in Inverness which was evidently blessed as Jock Troup returned the next month accompanied by Peter Connelly.

At this time, advertisements appeared under the name of Inverness YMCA Brotherhood. What the Inverness YMCA Brotherhood was is not certain. They advertised open meetings (for men and women) in the Wesleyan Central Hall (the former Music Hall on Union Street, just above the entrance to the public markets). A series of advertisements under the same name and for the same venue gives no indication of the relationship of this group to the YMCA itself.

In January of 1923, the same YMCA Brotherhood promoted a public Sunday afternoon meeting under the auspices of the Public Health Committee of the Town Council of Inverness. The speaker was T. G. Mackenzie, Esq., M.D., Medical Superintendent, Inverness District Asylum. He gave an address on the subject, "The Problem of Venereal Disease in Relation to the Physical and Moral Wellbeing of the Association." Sacred Music was rendered by the Orchestra.

Apart from an advertisement for a Jumble Sale, the YMCA was silent about the Brotherhood. On March 6, 1923, however, an advertisement called for a special meeting of YMCA members, to be held in their own rooms. The advertisement closed with two words in big block letters - BUSINESS IMPORTANT.

Unfortunately, no further information is available to answer the questions raised by the sudden emergence and subsequent disappearance of the Inverness YMCA Brotherhood, nor why they met at a different venue than the YMCA rooms. Perhaps some internal power struggle occurred and was finally resolved without anybody recording the details for posterity. Whatever the circumstances were, the ensuing history of Inverness YMCA shows that spiritual interests prevailed. The original aim of the YMCA, "to win souls for Christ," appears to have been reclaimed or preserved. And the Association entered a new era of outreach ministry to the growing town of Inverness.

Group of Ladies' Bible Class.

Mrs Jenny Martin.

Mrs MacKay.

Chapter Nine

Rev. W. R. MacKay

Newspaper records of YMCA activities are strangely limited from 1923 on into the mid-1930's. However, in the providence of God, first-hand information about Club activities has been provided by a retired minister who was involved with the YMCA from 1927 to 1930 and again after 1934. The man, W. R. Mackay, younger brother of the aforementioned John A. Mackay, is a well-known Invernessian who, after earning a B.Sc. at University abandoned his plans to be a pharmacist to follow God's call into church ministry. Following a long and distinguished career which included parish work, years of Forces chaplaincy, then hospital chaplaincy, Rev. W. R. Mackay has returned to Inverness, the town of his birth, the hallowed place of his conversion to the Lord Jesus Christ, and the arena of his pre-retirement seventeen-year ministry as Hospitals' chaplain.

In 1927, when W. R. Mackay started attending, the YMCA President was John Mackenzie who managed the Northern Counties Institute for the Blind and attended the West Parish church. "Also, I had a grand uncle, Duncan McGregor, who served on the YMCA Board when I was nine," Rev. Mackay reminisced. "Years after emigrating to Australia, he came home and bought a grocer's shop in Eastgate. A single man, Uncle Duncan stayed in our home until he died. He was an elder in West Church when Rev. Connell was minister. He was also very involved in the YMCA and through him I became interested."

Actually, young W. R. Mackay was brought into the Association through the Photographic Club, yet another enterprising effort to draw lads into the YMCA. Not everybody

appreciated the new paths struck by YMCA leaders in their
desire to win young men to Christ. W. R. Mackay remembered
a particular bone of contention which some older Christians
found hard to appreciate.

"In my day, billiards and snooker used to be associated with
the sleazier side of life," Mr. Mackay said. "In some people's
eyes it was a bit of a black mark on the YMCA for them to have
billiard tables."

Black mark or not, the billiard tables were installed and, for
many years, brought into the Club classes of boys who would
not normally have come. The personal work done by the
YMCA secretary and other members who were converted
themselves ensured that many of these boys found their way
beyond the billiard room to the good Gospel meetings held
every Sunday at eight o'clock. The same was true of lads who
came to the Mutual Improvement Society, or the Photographic
Club or any one of the other novel attractions organised to
interest young men who otherwise showed no initial desire to
attend religious meetings.

From 1927-30, before undertaking his four-year B.Sc. de-
gree, Mr. Mackay was an apprentice pharmacist in Inverness.
It was during this period that he spent a lot of time in the
YMCA rooms.

"The building occupied the corner of High Street and Castle
Street," Mr. Mackay recollected. "From the Castle Street
window I could look across to the new Town Hall and the
nearby cab-stand where usually two horse-drawn cabs waited
for hire. There were a few motor cars, but no traffic lights in
the town. From the High Street window I saw the Bank of
Scotland - no Woolworths in those days."

"The YMCA owned the whole building," Mr. Mackay
continued. "The whole ground floor was let out to two shops.
I remember one was Grant Clan Tartan, later Cameron's
clothing shop."

Young W. R. Mackay was converted during the three years of his apprenticeship in Inverness. He was brought into awareness of the Most High through the dark valley of deep sorrow.

"I spent the last day of my holidays in Aberdeen with a friend who attended college." Rev. Mackay remembers the details vividly. "We had a wonderful day of fellowship and fun. Back home the next morning, I was going to my work when I saw the headline, 'Aberdeen student in tragic accident'. I bought the paper and got the shock of my life. My friend's name leaped out at me. He had stepped off a bus and was hit by a cyclist. His skull was crushed and he died on the way to hospital. In the midst of my personal sorrow, the thought arrested me. 'What if that had been me'. I knew I was not ready. Through that accident, I was wakened to spiritual things, and God graciously led me to faith in the finished work of the Lord Jesus Christ."

The reality of God's work in W. R. Mackay's life was confirmed by Divine blessing upon his ministry. Having gone from University to the Free Church College in Edinburgh, the young ministry student spent his holidays in Inverness where he sometimes preached at the YMCA Sunday evening service.

"One evening, I spoke on Belshazzar and the writing on the wall." Rev. MacKay recalled. "Some time later, a young man told me that God had blessed him that evening." In the Providence of God, this young man was eventually led to study in the Free Church College and, upon completion of his studies, laboured faithfully as a Free Church minister until his home-call.

Another evening, after conducting the service at the YMCA the preacher was told a very rough-looking man wished to speak with him. The enquirer was a man about forty years old. That night, as he sought the Lord, he confessed that more than half of his life had been spent behind bars for just about every

crime except murder. He was a terror to those who knew him.
But that night, as W. R. Mackay and another YMCA member
shared the message of God's love in Jesus Christ, the seeking
man kneeled and cried to the Lord for forgiveness. He asked
for a Bible before returning to his lodgings at the Model on
Dunabban Street. Later, it was divulged by another Model
resident that the new convert read the Bible openly and went
on his knees to pray before the wondering eyes of his fellow-
lodgers. Nobody interfered - the man's fierce reputation
ensured that.

Wonderfully converted, the new Christian obtained employment in Dundee as a company representative for a Christian
business man. In the course of his travels, the man frequently
called at the Carrbridge Free Church manse where he enjoyed
fellowship with W. R. Mackay and his wife, the three speaking
together of the things of the Lord. In time, the man was happily
married and walked before the Lord for many years until his
death.

God's saving grace comes from God alone. But God uses
various agencies such as the YMCA as instruments of His
grace. Established in 1859 for the very purpose of winning
souls to Christ, the YMCA experienced, through conversions
like those described above, affirmation of the fundamental
reason for its existence. Heaven alone knows how many have
been converted through Inverness YMCA ministries - and
how much good has been done through those so converted. It
is enough that heaven knows. But let those who pray and work
for God through Inverness YMCA be encouraged by these
known trophies of grace.

W. R. Mackay moved from Carrbridge at the outbreak of
World War Two, joining the Cameronians as Army Chaplain.
(The Cameronians were the "Covenanting Regiment" from
the borders of Scotland, taking their name from famous
covenanter Richard Cameron. Now disbanded, the

Cameronians was the only regiment permitted to carry rifles on church parades.)

In Palestine the day peace was declared, Rev. MacKay recounts this story of that great event. "While visiting my friend who was minister of St. Andrew's Church of Scotland in Jerusalem, we heard more and more bells ringing. Then we saw troops from many regiments making their way up the hill to the church. Somebody called out the news and my minister friend said, 'We'll have to hold a service.' He asked me to preach. I will never forget the sense of gratitude to God which permeated that worship service."

An octogenarian at the time of writing, Rev. W. R. Mackay has officially retired from active ministry. Having preached in the YMCA of the late 1920's, Rev. Mackay still occasionally occupies the Sunday Evening service pulpit in the YMCA of 1992 - and still preaches the eternal Gospel of the Lord Jesus Christ, the message of which has brought hope and new life to so many who have passed through the hall of Inverness YMCA.

Group of Members with Rev. Wm. Still and Mr Archie Frame, 1963.

Group of Members with President Mr J. Macpherson, 1950's.

Chapter Ten

World War Two

The years following the Great War (and perhaps the years preceding it) seem to have worked a gradual erosion of membership in Inverness YMCA. Existing minutes show, with notable exceptions, less of the grand evangelistic zeal which marked the first four decades. Instead, the Committee's major preoccupation centred on how to raise money for operating costs. Discussion around the subject absorbed countless hours of urgent talk.

Thirty members turned out for the 1936 Annual General Meeting - a far cry from the 500 to 600 of the 1860's. The financial report for the preceding year, reproduced below, identifies some of the fund-raising projects. These included whist drives, cake and candy sales, flag days, jumble sales - all of which, added to the rent income from the two shops below the Rooms, subscription and user fees, private bath and canteen earnings, left the YMCA with a working loss of over sixteen pound.

The financial statement item "Miscellaneous (Concerts, Whist Drives, etc)" shows a cost of 16/4/6 and a total income of 15/10/11. Perhaps it was the loss factor which gave impetus to the formation of a "dance" sub-committee, the said committee being charged with the responsibility of setting up a dance in Burnett's Tearooms. Proposed by the joint-chairman of the Sports Committee, the idea was thoroughly researched. Minutes of March 18, 1937 contain lengthy information about the dance. The Board was told that the price would be 2/3 per couple if 60 couples attended. After itemizing the associated costs, the report finally states with that number of couples the expenditure would exceed income. A revised admission fee of

3/6 would realize a profit of two pounds. If 65 couples attended, the profit would soar to 3/7/6.

Allowing that a pound was a fair bit of money in those years, and that the financial need was pressing, it still seems that a potential two pounds profit was not much of a financial pay-off for departing from long-honoured principles of faith. This event appears to have marked a pivotal point in local YMCA activities. Inverness Christians knew Hudson Taylor's famous sentiment, "God's work, done God's way, will never lack God's provision." For many of the supporting churches (though not all) this departure was viewed as not being on the path of God's Will. Nevertheless, the dance was evidently held.

At the Committee meeting following the dance, it was reported that "there was still money for dance tickets to be collected." A fuller report was promised for the next meeting, but nothing appears in the minutes of that meeting. History has thus kept secret the margin of profit (or loss) which the grand project realized.

Though the dance subcommittee stayed silent, it was a gloomy financial report at the General Managment Committee of October 5, 1937. The operating overdraft of 300 pounds had been exceeded by 60 pounds. In what is reminiscent of attacking an elephant with a fly-swatter, the minutes direct that a letter be sent to Mr. R- "Temperance Organiser, with regard to table loaned for Temperance Fair which was returned with one leg broken and to intimate that same would have to be repaired at his expense."

Discussion was already underway for sale of the Rooms since it was the Board's view that the property (which had been built specifically for YMCA purposes) was not suitable for YMCA purposes. No details are provided, but since programme activities included a Physical Training Class, it may well be that the general thrust of new programmes planned by the Board of that day required different premises.

In March, 1937, the President's report lamented the low interest shown by Committee members to the extent that on occasions there was not present the quorum required to conduct lawful business. He also bemoans the lapse of a number of the committees including the Literary and Rifle club activities. The religious committee work under the convenorship of Mr. Hugh Masson received favourable mention, however, the fact being noted that the meetings held in the Hall on Sunday evenings were attracting large gatherings. The Dunain Mission was also doing well.

Perhaps the above is sufficient to suggest the milieu in which the Inverness YMCA found itself, and the generally secularized atmosphere which seemed to have been encroaching upon Club leadership.

In contrast, it should be noted that, at that time, the Scottish National Council arranged a Conference of the Northern Associations of YMCA's in Inverness, the printed programme for which reminded members of The Founder's Legacy, from George Williams, reprinted from the British Y.M.C.A. Review.

"My last legacy, and it is a precious one, is the Young Men's Christian Association. I leave it to you, beloved young men of many countries, to carry on and extend."

"In fulfillment of that prophecy of the preciousness of his legacy the Young Men's Christian Association today stands as one of the greatest agencies in the world for the building of Christ's Kingdom and of Christ-like characters, next to the schools and colleges as a great educational factor, one of the leaders of the world in physical education and development, and with few rivals in breaking down the barriers set up by the diverse creeds, castes, and cultures throughout the earth, thus making it a powerful factor for world peace. But the inscription will not really be fulfilled while young men around the world are not assuming the responsibility he (George Williams) left them, to carry on and extend the work of the Association."

The Conference did not seem to change the motivation levels of the Association Committee members. Poor attendance of members at subsequent business meetings and Sunday evening meetings is noted. Although the Sunday evening service was apparently flourishing, in June of 1939 a motion was made to discontinue Sunday services for the summer months. The motion succeeded over the objections of Mr. Masson and Mr. D. Walker.

At the outbreak of World War Two, Charles Young, who had just joined the committee, resigned to enter the Forces in the Medical Corps. Charles was one of countless young men responding to the call of "King and Country." The YMCA itself was once again pressed into service as a centre to serve His Majesty's Forces. This effectively interrupted the Club's financial problems and suspended further action concerning the sale of their property.

An article in the Inverness Courier, July 30, 1991, summarizes well the YMCA's work during the War. The article is reproduced below by kind permission of Inverness Courier.

Home From Home For The Forces.

During World War II, the YMCA had a major role to play in the provision of "home comforts" for the troops, in this country and overseas.

In Inverness they had operated a canteen from the YMCA Institute at the bottom of Castle Street since the outbreak of war, and also provided limited accommodation. But by 1941 the need for more beds for the increasing numbers of troops passing through the town had become acute.

The YMCA was invited to help, and the result was the formation of the Inverness YMCA War Emergency Committee, under the chairmanship of Provost Hugh Mackenzie.

Within a short time the committee had acquired the lease of Victor Conn's Restaurant at 24 High Street, and the three flats above it. The aim was to turn the Castle Street premises into a hostel, and to transfer the canteen to the Conn d'Or which was to become a restaurant and social centre for members of all the Services. The rooms above were also to be converted into sleeping accommodation for a further 100 servicemen.

The work seems to have been completed in a matter of weeks. The redecoration work was paid for by an anonymous donor, and the cost of furnishing one of the dormitories was met by the Canadian YMCA, in gratitude for the facilities offered to Canadians in the town. Over-all financial responsibiliity for the project rested, however, with the Scottish National Council of the YMCA.

The official opening was performed by the Prime Minister of New Zealand, Peter Fraser, who was in the Highlands to visit the house at Fearn in which he was born.

The new hostel helped ease what had become an accommodation crisis for the large numbers of servicemen travelling through Inverness - at that time the hub of a vast "Protected Area" covering the Highlands. Men had sometimes had to sleep in the open because of the shortage of beds.

Merchant seamen and members of Allied forces were also able to use the hostel and its facilities, which included a reading room. There was a small paid staff, but a large band of volunteers was needed to run the hostel, and there were repeated appeals for more helpers - men as well as women - to work in the canteen and to make beds. The day-to-day running of the hostel was in the hands of a "General Committee of Ladies" chaired by Baroness Burton.

Within months, however, it became clear an extension would be required and the next-door premises were acquired for a recreation room. Linked to the hostel by a covered way, this was opened in January 1942 and was equipped with a piano and games such as darts and bagatelle. Again, the Courier's columns were used to appeal for donations of furniture such as easy chairs and bookcases. There were also plans to provide 30 more beds, as well as a rest room and showers.

During the dark days of the war countless thousands of British and Allied servicemen were grateful for the warmth and comfort provided by the "YM" in their High Street home from home.

The YMCA does not nowadays (1990's) have as high a profile as some other charities and voluntary organisations, but some ideas of the vast scope of its wartime work throughout the world can be gleaned from the Inverness Courier's coverage of 50 years ago.

The Inverness hostel and restaurant was only one of 1000 centres opened by the YMCA since the beginning of the war including 10 in the Middle East and one in Tobruk.

"Among its many activities the YMCA includes the provision of over 800 mobile canteens in this country alone, and is responsible for the canteen service on trains between Edinburgh and London and Glasgow and London," the Courier reported.

"Of particular interest to us in the North is the important part played by the YMCA in looking after the welfare of our prisoners of war. There are six field secretaries of whom four are Swedes, one Swiss and one American, who visit prison camps in Germany regularly, and have done a great deal to promote educational and social functions in these camps. Recently the YMCA was asked to provide fifteen sets of bagpipes for prisoners of war and already several sets have been donated."

Chapter Eleven

Expropriation - and Poverty

At the end of the World War Two, the whole Western world faced the massive task of converting to a peacetime economy. Inverness YMCA was not excluded from this requirement. Although government authorities did not immediately relinquish control of the properties, the Association's Board of Management resumed proceedings to dispose of the building. In 1945, the YMCA tested the market for the value of its property (a prime location in the very centre of the town's retail and commercial section) and immediately received four offers, the largest being 39,900 pounds submitted by Marks and Spencer's. On the strength of the latter offer, the Inverness YMCA Board, with the advice and initial bridge financing of the National YMCA, purchased the Palace Hotel on Ardross Terrace for 35,000 pounds, a fair 1945 market value. Unfortunately, coincident with the purchase, a new national law entitled the Town and County Planning Act gave the Inverness Town Council power to acquire ownership of the property - a power they exercised with dispatch. The YMCA was informed its property would be expropriated, ostensibly to effect demolition so as to widen the junction of High Street and Castle Street. The government assessor was to evaluate the YMCA property at 1939 prices.

Many years were to pass before the actual street widening took place - and the Town Council's resale of the property, far from being 1939 prices, was for an amount which rightfully should have gone to the on-going work of the YMCA.

No evidence exists to prove that opportunistic local business and civic leaders took advantage of the YMCA in acquiring the premises for a depressed price only to sell for a large price (not to mention keeping Marks and Spencer's or some similar chain from obtaining strategic commercial property) but the facts recorded in the minutes of the Town Council meetings of the day point to injustice and still plead for redress in the form of adequate financial compensation to the YMCA. Moral suasion failed to alter the circumstances at the time, however, and these matters may well have to be left to the judgment of history - and to the judgment of the Almighty Himself.

(Years later, at the opening of the new YMCA building on Bank Street in 1969, the then Provost Smith said, "... (the Castle Street building) became a casualty to modern planning. I realize, ladies and gentlemen, I've got to be careful what I say and as the present Provost of Inverness I would not wish to dwell on that particular transaction. But I am bound to say that in all ways the town of Inverness owes a debt to the YMCA and you can be assured that as long as I am a member of that council we will not forget that we are indebted to the YMCA tremendously.")

In fairness to Inverness Town Council, it should be noted that, when the matter was raised some years later, small donations from the town were forwarded to the YMCA for a few years after the expropriation. A YMCA business minute of December 12, 1976 states that the Inverness Town Council normally sends 80 to 100 pounds per annum as a donation to YMCA activities. A sensitive conscience would note that this amount is a mere percentage of the interest earned on the profit the Town realized upon the sale of the YMCA Castle Street Building.

To avoid saddling the future YMCA leaders with an unmanageable debt-load, the 1945 Committee decided to sell the Palace Hotel immediately after acquiring it. That appears to have been a wise foresight. Fortunately, the Palace Hotel resale reflected the rapidly rising property prices and a profit of almost five hundred pounds was realized on the resale. This amount paled into insignificance against the real loss to the YMCA when the District Evaluator stated that he found himself "unable to recommend that the Town Council pay any higher compensation than 10,500 pounds as fair and full compensation for the subjects concerned." In the absence of any realistic option, the YMCA Board of Management was obliged to accept the offer.

The Town Council permitted the YMCA to remain in the Rooms for the next few years until demolition of the building in 1951. However, this largesse was largely spoiled by the requirement that the YMCA pay rent to the new official owners (namely, the Town Council). And, it was not easy for the YMCA as tenants to get maintainance repairs attended to with the same despatch the Council showed in acquiring ownership.

Members at Garden Party in St Margaret's in 1959.

Back row — David Morrison, John Fraser, Joe MacKenzie, Duncan Urquhart. Seated — Rodrick Morrison, Tom Macdonald, John Mackenzie. Taken in the late 1950's.

Group of Members with Rev. Wm Still and Mr A. Frame.

Chapter Twelve
Converted In Jerusalem

The work of God continued in spite of the seeming setbacks. In April, 1948, a young man, recently demobilized from the Army, had entered the doors of YMCA for the first time. Coming specifically to hear a speaker whom he had previously met during military service in the Middle East, Thomas John MacDonald could not have had any idea that his first step into the Inverness YMCA was the beginning of a life-long ministry which spans forty-five years and still continues at date of writing.

Mr. S. F. Cupples was the speaker that night. A missionary with The Mission To Mediterranean Garrisons, Mr. Cupples and his wife had been richly blessed in their ministry to servicemen and women, conducted out of a hut in the Allenby Barracks in Jerusalem. More than a thousand recorded conversions occurred in that hut during the War years alone, where Mr. and Mrs Cupples served tea and showed slides to the soldiers. One night in May, 1947, attracted by the tea and Mrs Cupple's home-baking, young Lance Corporal Tom MacDonald entered the hut. Watching the slides, he noticed the words of a hymn which was being illustrated. The hymn was,

> At even, ere the sun was set
> The sick O Lord around Thee lay
> Oh with what diverse needs they met
> Oh with what joy they went away.

After the slides, Mr. Cupples gave a brief Gospel message through which the Lord spoke to Tom. Quietly, the young lad from Inverness bowed his head and sought the Lord. Afterwards, Tom spoke with Mr. Cupples who counselled him further from Scripture. Just at the midnight hour (often the darkest hour in human experience) the seeking soldier found light and life in Jesus Christ.

Tom became a close personal friend of Mr. and Mrs. Cupples and began to grow in the things of the Lord as they ministered to him. The friendship continued when Tom returned to Civvie Street. Thus, in 1948, when Mr. Cupples was booked to speak at Inverness YMCA, Tom was there to hear him.

Tom joined Inverness YMCA just at a time when that organisation was sensing the need to reclarify its central mission. Some of the office-bearers, including Mr. Masson (president) had held the fort since before the Second World War and were waiting for younger members to take up the reins of leadership. Tom was promptly drafted on to the Management Committee where he sat for two years, helping as he could but also analyzing what needed to change for God's Work to prosper in the Club.

Tom's zeal as a new Christian was matched by a native ability to make things happen. Of course, making things happen required a hundred percent determination and effort. Tom personified the "one percent inspiration, ninety-nine percent perspiration" approach. He was neither haphazard nor slothful in his way of doing things. And, he drew the best out of others by example and by straightforward challenge when that was necessary.

Mr. Cupples had counselled Tom MacDonald well. Theologically sound yet unbound by tradition, Tom's Christianity was one which "wore overalls", which got its hands dirty, which put the advance of the work before personal pride. That's why Tom, too fiercely independent to ever ask anybody for anything for himself, was able and willing to beg, borrow or sometimes coerce from others time and material help for the benefit of Inverness YMCA.

Something of the general atmosphere prevailing at Inverness YMCA during the two years leading up to his election as Secretary can be gleaned from the Minutes. For example, in November, 1948, the Minutes show that a motion was put forward to cancel the Sunday evening meetings because of "rowdy-ism". The Sunday evening meeting was probably the main point of interaction between the Christian public and the YMCA and had been running for a hundred years. God had used that meeting time and time again to call people to Himself through Christ, and to challenge Christians to deeper consecration. The Sunday evening After Church Rally was, in a very real sense, the heart-throb of the Club. Now a call came for its cancellation.

The motion was defeated, and a motion of a different spirit was put forward. This motion required that members would only be admitted to the Association at a "devotional and dedication" service.

Soon after, a firm policy was struck which forbade letting the premises for dances. Surprisingly, a motion was then put forward by a long-serving previous religious committee convener suggesting dancing on Saturday evenings "for members only". This was soundly defeated and the former religious convenor resigned from the office he now held.

The Annual General Meeting of 1949 saw the resignation of the President, Mr. Masson. A motion was made that he be elected an Honorary President but an amendment that the matter be remitted to the new Committee was tabled and nothing further was heard of the intention.

During the preceding year (1948) some seven boys had taken a definite Christian stand. The Annual Report also showed that the Sunday evening services were progressing favourably and the Dunain Mission Sunday School was flourishing but the Sunday evening services there were poorly attended. The provision of supporting funds from the Inverness YMCA was proving to be a financial drain. The possibility of selling Dunain Mission was discussed.

Dunain Mission Superintendent at that time was Mr. Donald Davidson. He replaced Mr. Fraser, who had cared for Dunain Mission assisted by Mr. Walter and Mr. Ross who also conducted a Sunday School at Culduthel. (Mr. and Mrs. Ross's daughter, Catherine, is the wife of Alister C. MacDonald, Wester Inches, who served as religious convener in Inverness YMCA in 1951.)

Messrs. Fraser, Walter and Ross had met most of the costs of Dunain mission at their own expense for many years; a practice which Mr. Davidson emulated. Along with Peter MacGregor, Donald Davidson was nominated to the position of President in 1949, but he did not allow his name to stand, leaving Mr. Peter MacGregor to be elected by acclamation.

Many of these men were relatively new to the Management Committee. Amongst them were those who represented a fresh wave of dedication to the primary aims of the YMCA. Other names which appeared for the first time during the 1949/50 period are Hugh Mackay and David Fraser, Bible teacher J. A. Ferrier, Rev. C. P. Smith and Rev. John MacBeath. Rev. MacBeath (minister of Inverness Baptist Church) had a good work among youth through the Saturday night meeting which had gone on throughout the war and was the scene of much spiritual blessing. This godly man was fully occupied with growing ministries in his church as well as a personal soul-winning ministry and obviously could not give the YMCA his time, though he gave it his unqualified support. It was a time for change, and God was leading to the work those whom He had chosen to lead the Club into a new era.

The elections of March, 1951 Annual General Meeting installed a new slate of officers to the Management Committee, including Donald Davidson as president and T. J.

Chapter Thirteen

Moving "Down" - To Bank Street

When the YMCA was finally required to move out of its premises on Castle Street, Mrs. Jenny Martin kindly gave the use of a property she owned. It was only a small room on the side of Raining Stairs, but it gave respite while suitable premises were sought. Ashvale, the old St. Columba Church manse on Culduthel Road, was made available for the very reasonable price of 4,000 pounds and Club operations (including hostel services) were centred in the large house on Culduthel Road.

In 1953, the YMCA purchased an old building on Bank Street (site of the present building) for 4,000 pounds. Although it was 150 years old, the layout of the building was suitable for Club purposes, having a large upstairs hall which could seat around 250. Downstairs, a large hall served as games room with two smaller rooms, one becoming the office and lounge for the nucleus members (Christians) and the other serving as canteen/library for the general public who participated in the sports and other Club activities.

The years 1953 to 1960 were a time of rebuilding spiritually. Focussing on this, Tom spent every free hour at the Club or doing Club business. Somehow, he always came up with the money to obtain furniture, pay for food supplies, and provide sweeties for distribution on Sunday afternoon when the YMCA boys unfailingly visited the elderly residents of Muirfield Hospital Sometimes a visiting speaker had to be placed in overnight accommodation. Tom made sure the bill was paid. It was a time when Inverness YMCA itself had very little money - indeed, very little of anything except faith and joy in the Lord.

"People gave us old furniture for the lounge," Tom commented. "I also remember a time when we saw a bunch of records somebody had put in their bucket. We waited until it was dark, then snatched the lot."

Another time, the buckets yielded a haul of cups, saucers and plates, even a tea-pot, cast-offs from some Inverness citizen who had either risen in affluence or passed on to a state where kitchen dishes were of no further use. For years afterwards, these dishes were well used in the Club on Bank Street. In fact, we got so much stuff for the Club out of other people's cast-off rubbish that it got to be pretty hard for us to pass a bucket if the lid was on.

We also became the recipients of cast-off furniture. On one occasion in 1956, Hetty MacPherson, who owned a general store at the top of Castle Street, bought a chesterfield suite at auction for one shilling. Alister Cameron and some of the other lads helped to roll the chesterfield from Castle Street down to the Club on Bank Street. The wheels kept coming off, which made the trip a difficult one. In those days, the Club also boasted ownership of a couple of chairs made out of beer barrels. The incongruence of their origin didn't seem to bother any of the Club members. We were grateful for something relatively comfortable to sit on.

In those days, because the boys at the YMCA didn't have much, they looked forward with added expectation when a prominent speaker was invited. Usually, after a meeting, the members gathered in the lounge to consume large quantities of thickly-sliced toast and jam. When a special speaker came, however, the boys dug deep into their pockets to buy cakes from Anderson the Bakers. "We always got much more than we paid for," Tom acknowledged.

Part of Tom's analysis of the Club activities had been a

recognition that the Word of God and prayer must be central to all its endeavours. A public voluntary organisation like the YMCA always stands in danger of attracting people whose aim was to build their own kingdom or advance their own interests. Also, there had always been individuals in the Club who wanted to stress the sports and social sides of the Red Triangle (YMCA worldwide symbol) to the detriment of the spiritual. Tom saw clearly that this was a fundamental struggle, and he determined that the God Whom He served would have first place in Inverness YMCA. Tom's constant prayer, expressed frequently in public prayer meetings and conversation with other members was actually a Biblical prayer - "Lead me in the way everlasting." Encouraging others who shared this desire to become members, Tom finally saw the opposition voted out of office and men of faith and commitment voted in.

Though there were some rich men associated with the Club, the financial needs continued. In November, 1951, the Board moved that a house to house collection be held on behalf of the YMCA. Also, sales of work were conducted and a list of prominent citizens were invited to become Honorary Presidents - a yearly donation being expected from each one who accepted. The little bit of income thus generated made no practical difference to the Club's financial state. In those early years of Tom's leadership, part of the price of keeping spiritually-minded people in office meant the withdrawal of many who could have helped a great deal financially. Believing that "the cattle on a thousand hills are His," and willing to lay their own wallets on the altar of service, the members somehow kept things going. Meanwhile, God began to give fruit as young men were converted and started to "grow in grace and in the knowledge of (their) Lord and Saviour, Jesus Christ."

In 1956, both in Inverness YMCA and throughout the town,

there was a spiritual awareness reminiscent of the period when
Moody and Sankey ministered in the town almost eighty years
before. The 1953 Billy Graham Harringay Evangelistic Crusade had made a huge impression on the City of London,
indeed on the whole British Isles. Tom, along with Billy
Mitchell, Charles Young, Donald Davidson, George Burgess
and Jimmy Sutherland, had travelled to London at the time and
sensed the power of God in the preached Word.

Inverness YMCA garnered fruit from the 1955 Tell Scotland
movement. The general interest in American evangelist Billy
Graham aroused by the media resulted in record crowds
gathering under the sound of the Gospel, and a new liberty in
"gossiping the Gospel" in the work place. Young Christians
who worked at Macrae and Dick's garage (Jim Scobbie and
Derek Morrison) invited as many of their fellow-workmen as
they could to come to the evangelistic meetings being relayed
from Kelvin Hall into local churches. Many young people
were saved and some of the young men found their way into
the YMCA, bringing a new challenge for ministry to the
Committee there.

The efforts to organise a one-day visit to Inverness by Dr.
Billy Graham were joined to those of Inverness Christian
Businessmen Committee under the chairmanship of Donald
Davidson, and the meeting took place in Bught park. Over
20,000 people attended, many travelling from remote Highland places to be there. Billy Graham's message, delivered
with the evangelist's characteristic evangelistic zeal, concluded with "an appeal" for sinners to put their trust in the
finished work of the Lord Jesus Christ. More than six hundred
conversions were recorded that day.

It may be proper to speak of both the Harringay and Kelvin
Hall crusades as part of one great season of blessing the
Almighty was pleased to send to the United Kingdom. In
1953, for example, a young High School student named James

Scobbie was saved in Inverness. He recalls the period as one in which pre-evangelism was done by the YMCA and primarily through the personal soulwinning ministry of its secretary. Following his conversion, Mr. Scobbie became one of the nucleus of workers serving the Lord through the YMCA. In 1957, Mr. Scobbie and two other recent converts associated with the "YM" enrolled at Winnipeg Bible Institute and College of Theology in Manitoba, Canada, as a prelude to a church pastoral ministry which eventually elevated Rev. J. Scobbie to the Moderator's chair of the Evangelical Free Church of Canada.

Alister Cameron, who also completed studies at Winnipeg Bible Institute, has an interesting testimony of his involvement with the YMCA. After the Billy Graham meetings, Alister became exercised about his own spiritual condition. He went to see John Reid, a Methodist minister, who explained the way of salvation to him. Shortly after, Al found his way to the Club where he quickly became a diligent worker for the Lord.

Al recalls that he and some other lads became interested in Bible College training following the visit of a group from Wheaton College, Illinois. Al wrote to Trinity College, Florida, for information. The reply finally caught up with him in Winnipeg, Canada, where he, along with Jim Scobbie and Ed. Hughes, had enrolled as students. A former Sunday School teacher in a Gospel Hall in Swan Lane, Inverness, Alister soon became busily involved in assembly life at St. James Chapel, Winnipeg, where he holds a responsible ministry position at the time of writing.

To return to the Inverness of 1955. Girls were being saved as well as young men. Mr. Ferrier was encouraged to take responsibility for the Friday night Bible study, and the meeting was opened for both young men and young women. Thereafter, about thirty to forty women attended the Bible class. Many of these also helped out in fund-raising activities such as sales of work and teas. Notable among those women for commitment to the YMCA which proved to be long-term is Norma Mackenzie. For four decades now, Norma has stood behind the Club, supporting every effort.

In 1956, Donald Davidson declined to let his name stand for re-election as President. He was succeeded by W. (Billy) Mitchell, a member of the YMCA, who served in that office for two years. The Billy Graham meetings having brought in new converts who were now mature enough to serve on the Committee, the roster of the March, 1956 Management Committee meeting contained fifteen names as follows: W. Mitchell (chair); Messrs. A. Cameron, J. Mackenzie, R. Morrison, J. Scobbie, R. Hughes, J. Munro, J. Ferrier, W. Urquhart, G. Wilson, K. Martin, T. MacDonald, E.Hughes, H. Mitchell, C. Young. Apologies were received from Hugh Mackay and Davie Fraser.

There is no question that a new era commenced with the appointment of T. J. MacDonald as Secretary in 1951. In the providence of God, Tom's unpaid ministry was to continue until his official withdrawal from the office of honorary secretary in October, 1976, after which he remained as a Club Committee member, an active friend and an esteemed consultant. This period in the history of Inverness YMCA was richly eventful, and the verifiable records are so plentiful, that the era will be noted in yet more detail.

Chapter Fourteen

Saved and Growing

In the YMCA, Tom MacDonald's zeal and organisational leadership skills were matched by his ability to come alongside a prospective convert and share in practical ways the love of God and, eventually, the terms of the saving Gospel. No records exist of the number of young men who were thus led to the Saviour or built up in their most holy faith through this instrumentality - but the number is legion. Perhaps the author may be permitted to jump forward a few years and give his own testimony to the way in which God used Tom in his life.

"It was the evening of April 15, 1955. To my own surprise I found myself sitting under the sound of the Gospel in the old Union Street Music Hall, now the Methodist church. The preacher was Billy Graham, addressing a meeting at Kelvin Hall, Glasgow, with the service being relayed via land-lines to the remotest parts of the country. It is hardly an exaggeration to say that the whole of Scotland was listening in to Dr. Graham that night.

I knew Tom MacDonald as a fellow-employee working at Macrae and Dick's. Often I had benefitted from his generosity but, until that evening, my heart was shut tight to the things of God.

There was nothing in my background which would encourage anybody to see in me a prospective convert. Twice, as an early teenager, I had appeared before the court charged with theft. On each occasion I received a sentence of two years probation. Not only so, but I had learned to express myself in what I mistakenly thought of as 'man's language.' All in all, I was a most unlikely candidate for conversion.

Yet, I found myself in the Tell Scotland Evangelistic Crusade meeting the night of April 13th, 1955. In fact, I had been there the previous evening and sensed a momentary wistfullness as I watched others go forward in response to the Gospel invitation. Something drew me back to the next night's meeting - something I now know to be the gracious convicting work of the Holy Spirit, Who was a stranger to me at that time.

At the close of the service that evening, after a brief inward struggle, I went forward in tears and found myself confronted with verses from the Word of God which assured me of His love and acceptance in Christ. I was counselled by George Gill from Ebenezer Gospel Hall, who especially directed me to John 5:24 from whence God gave an assurance of my own personal salvation which has remained with me ever since. I was truly converted that evening and, though without much knowledge of Christian things, I knew my life was changed.

When I finally left the counselling room, (the last one to do so and therefore leaving an almost deserted church) I was stopped by a lone figure who stepped out of the shadows near the stone staircase. It was Tom MacDonald. He had seen me go forward, and waited to speak to me. Thrusting out his hand, he said, "Here. This is for you." It was a Personal Worker's New Testament, suitably inscribed with the words, "To Eddie. This Book will keep you from sin. Sin will keep you from this Book."

Immediately after my conversion Tom and others were there to introduce me to the YMCA and help me ease my way into the new life. Their wisdom and patience helped me through spiritual struggles as I faced the implications of no longer living for self. Along with Jimmy Scobbie and Alister Cameron (two other new converts of that time period) I met John MacKenzie, a couple of years younger than me but a true encourager with his warm smile and frankness of expression. Derek Morrison also encouraged me, as we worked together at MacRae and Dick's and sometimes had opportunity to talk.

Then there was Duncan Urquhart, John Fraser, Joe Munro, and George Wilson. Later, my own brother, Ronnie Hughes and a good number of younger lads became involved with the Club. Together, we entered into a new experience of learning to walk before the Lord. I became immersed in YMCA activities and spent most of my time there. At the same time, young boys were coming to the games room for table tennis and billiards. Among them were George and Donald MacAskill, twins who rose to championship status as a Badminton doubles team, but who forfeited a likely champion title because they refused to play the finals on the Lord's Day. Both these boys were later called into ministry. At the time of writing, George serves as minister of the Associated Presbyterian Church in Dumbarton, and Donald in a sister church in Dundee.

During the two years I spent at the Club before leaving for Canada, I appreciated that there was never a day when Tom was not available to act as mentor, encourager, sometimes gentle rebuker. I recall that Tom always maintained a level of integrity and honesty which I had never seen before. This special relationship Tom had with all the new Christians at the YMCA helped me until I, along with Jim Scobbie and Alister Cameron, left Inverness in 1957 to attend Winnipeg Bible Institute and College of Theology.

In those two years from my conversion in 1955 to 1957, I shared fully in the life of Inverness YMCA. Other young Christians were a great help to me. and Tom was always there, too, making sure all the boys were present at Club activities, giving us assignments such as leading the meeting, opening in prayer, ordering tracts, or procuring sweeties to pass out to the residents of two Care Homes we visited every Sunday. I was given pragmatic advice, too. Knowing of my previous track record of romantic involvement with the opposite sex, it was recommended to me in none too subtle terms that I would probably enjoy more rapid spiritual growth if I gave myself a year free from any special relationship. I must say that I was so entranced by the Bible truths I was discovering that the advice didn't seem the least bit hard. In the event, I ultimately left for Canada unencumbered emotionally, and found to my delight that there, in the Bible School student body, God had somebody who became a wonderful wife to me. But, I digress.

As I recall, in 1955 to 1957 we had Missionary Prayer meeting on Monday; Men's Bible Class on Tuesday; our church prayer meeting on Wednesday; a free night on Thursday (which meant an evening of happy fellowship at the YMCA); a mixed Bible study on Friday; Open Air meetings on the Exchange on Saturday; Visitation to Ach-an-eas and Muirfield Hospital every Sunday afternoon to distribute sweeties, read and pray with the residents, and offer tracts. Muirfield Hospital was the former Town Poorhouse and still retained much of the Dickens-like atmosphere when the YMCA boys first started their regular weekly vistis. Miss Mary Shaw, then a young nurse at Muirfield, became a life-long friend and supporter of the YMCA.

Also, of course, the Sunday Night After Church rally continued. All of us had to take our turn chairing the meeting.

By ten o'clock each evening the meetings were over and the boys gathered in the front room around a monstrous tea-pot and a mountain of toast. Raspberry jam made by the YMCA boys completed the feast. Then we would stroll home in a group, everybody walking together to drop off the first person, then the next. Tom was always the last of the bunch, the one who walked home alone. I reckon that he walked an average of five miles every night. It's hard to believe, but during these late-night walks the subject of our sometimes clamorous discussion was most often a complex theological truth which was chewed over, kicked over, and argued over until every conceivable side of the question had been covered. It was a great way of learning the facts of Scripture - and how to think logically and recognize when others weren't.

Members also developed a YMCA camping programme. We used primitive gear and had very basic food supplies. But we were young men full of fun and eager to lean into life. Somehow, Tom always managed to scrounge the loan of somebody's car (not many working class people had cars in those days). Everybody was glad to let Tom be the spokesman when we camped one day on a wee tree-sheltered meadow at the side of the road far from any living being (we thought) only to be ordered off the land as trespassers by the haughty owner who gave us fifteen minutes to get off her land. Good days, these were, when a carload of young Christians would motor down to Edinburgh to visit the Danson-Smith family, then return by way of Aberdeen to catch Mr. Still's worship service at Gilcomston South Church of Scotland.

Perhaps this is a good time to highlight the privileged relationship which the YMCA boys shared with Mr. and Mrs. Danson-Smith and their family. Mrs. Danson-Smith was formerly a missionary in Jerusalem; Mr. Danson-Smith owned a book-publishing business in Edinburgh from where he distributed Bibles and Christian literature all over the world. A well-known poet, Mr. Danson-Smith also emphasized Biblical truths in all his poetry.

In the providence of God, the Inverness YMCA boys and the Danson-Smith family became firm friends. The Danson-Smiths, both Godly people, showed a keen (and generous) interest in the Club, on one occasion gifting each of the boys an Amplified New Testament.

When Mr. Danson-Smith died, although he was very well-known throughout the circle of Scottish Christian leadership, it was the boys from the Inverness YMCA who were asked to be pall-bearers at his funeral. For years afterwards, the YM boys visited Mrs. Danson-Smith until God called this gracious

lady to join the "general assembly of the firstborn" in the
heavenly home to which her husband had preceded her.

At the time of writing, Grace Danson-Smith and her brother
Theodore are carrying on the publishing and book distribution
started by their father. We record our thanks to them for
permission to reproduce Mr. Danson-Smith's poem, one
which was a great favourite in Inverness YMCA.

I Cannot Tell

*"Who His own self bare our sins in His own body on the tree" (1 Peter
2:24)*

I cannot tell why this world was created -
The blessed Book makes not this problem clear;
One thing I know, it cannot be debated,
And that is this - the fact that I am here.
And when I leave this earth, where shall I go?
That surely is the thing I ought to know.

I cannot tell why sin was found in heaven;
Nor can I solve the mystery of the fall;
But oh, I know mankind can be forgiven
If on the Lord for pardon they will call;
For all man's sin and guilt Christ fully bore
That man to his first place He might restore.

I cannot tell about the wondrous glory
Of that celestial Home - surpassing fair;
Nor yet depict the awesome, tragic story
Of life in hell, in hopeless, dark despair;
But this I know - there's life for every one
Who will accept, as Saviour, God's dear Son.

As young Christians, we had many great advantages during
these years at the YMCA. For one thing, we sat under the

ministry of gifted teachers - not only the internationally famous like William Still of Aberdeen and James Philip of Edinburgh, but also from Mr. J. A. Ferrier, and Mr. George Mackenzie, (both in fellowship at local assemblies) as well as many Highland clergymen who excelled in teaching the Word of God. Just as a child acquires the major proportion of language in the first four years of his life so, I believe, in these early years at the Inverness YMCA we young Christians absorbed a major proportion of the Christian truth which formed the foundation of our future lives.

Most of us younger Christians in Inverness YMCA received our first practical training in preaching through participating in open air meetings and leading the Sunday evening services. For myself, I must say it stood me and my two friends in good stead when we left the sheltered environment of the YMCA to go to Canada. My two colleagues and I were immediately useful to the church we associated with there, and became very active as soon as we arrived

Besides head knowledge of the Scriptures and technical how-to's of Christian ministry, I received from the YMCA boys' modelling of practical "agape" love a precious legacy which forever endears to my heart the old Club on Bank Street, Inverness. Not only so, but Tom's consistent friendship has spanned the ocean and spanned the years. I'm sure the YMCA motto "All One In Christ Jesus" has never been more clearly felt than it is amongst the fraternity of Christians who have passed through the special fellowship of Inverness YMCA - and especially those who have been the objects of Tom MacDonald's committed ministries.

John Fraser, mentioned above, was one "object of Tom MacDonald's committed ministries." John is also an example of God's grace in the life of a young man who subsequently experienced spiritual growth through the YMCA. John's mother died when he was twelve and the family of five had to be dispersed among relatives for a few years. Back home at age fifteen, John was impressed by the testimony of his younger sister Annette who had been saved during the Billy Graham meetings.

John noted the difference Christ made to Annette's life and began to listen to Gospel broadcasts over Radio Luxembourg. One night, Charles E. Fuller quoted the text, "He that hath the Son, hath life. He that hath not the Son of God hath not life. (1 John 5:12). This Word brought John to faith and he started a new life in Christ.

John came into the YMCA in 1956 and was soon a regular participant in the Bible studies, prayer meetings, and other Club activities. In the Club he met Evelyn Riddoch who had been converted at a YMCA Bible study led by S. F. Cupples of The Mission To Mediterranean Garrisons.

In time, John and Evelyn married and eventually made their home in Aberdeen. They have been associated with the Gilcomston South Church of Scotland for the past twenty-two years, where John is now an elder.

Wilfred Urquhart, whose conversion story opens this book, was also one of those "objects of Tom MacDonald's committed ministries". We now return to Wilfred's involvement in the YMCA in the years which followed his new birth into Christian life.

Chapter Fifteen

Training For World Mission

The night after Wilfred Urquhart was saved he entered the YMCA with a new identity. Wilf was now "a son of God through faith in Jesus Christ."(Galatians 3:26.) Like the other young Christians there, Wilfred soon found that the YMCA served as a second home to him. He was there every night, becoming one of the regulars. Wilf attended the Bible Classes without fail, finding in the Scriptures the spiritual food which helped him to "grow in grace and in the knowledge of (his) Lord and Saviour, Jesus Christ." (II Peter 3:18.)

"It didn't take me long to get immersed in the YMCA outreach ministries," Wilfred disclosed. "I gave my testimony at an Open Air Meeting we held on Saturdays at the Town Exchange. We also distributed tracts. Then, on Saturday nights, we used to go to the Locarno cafe to buy sweeties for distribution to the old ladies at Muirfield Institution." Wilf laughed. "Sometimes it was quite a temptation not to scoff the sweeties ourselves on Saturday night. We had to make do with thick slices of toasted bread and Tom's raspberry jam."

Gradually, Inverness YMCA became central to Wilfred's life, a focal point for fellowship and service to God. During normal Club evenings, he played table tennis, billiards and darts with the young boys who came to the games room, befriending them, praying for them and seeking to influence them for Christ as others had sought to influence him. Since his post office duties allowed him a forty-five minute break in mid-morning, Wilf used that time to slip down to the Club rooms where he vacuumed and dusted and generally cleaned up. This quickly became part of Wilfred's daily schedule, a labour of love and gratitude to God Who had lifted him "out of a fearful pit and from the miry clay", and put "a new song" in his mouth, and established his goings. (Psalm 40)

An early start meant that Wilfred's work day was completed by early afternoon. "Then I'd finish tidying up at the Club and get things ready for the evening," he reported. "I did major cleaning projects in that time slot, too. Over time, I polished years of neglect off the stairs, getting the shine to a decent level, then doing them regularly to keep the stairs at a high gleam."

Wilfred didn't mind doing the humble work of an unpaid custodian. Quietly, drawing no attention to himself, he spent those hours alone in the building, polishing on hands and knees the huge games room, the smaller rooms, the stairs and large meeting hall. As he scrubbed and polished, perhaps Wilfred hummed the words of a hymn he'd heard for the first time at the Club.

"Saviour, Thy dying love,
Thou gavest me.
Nor should I ought withhold, My Lord from Thee.
In love my soul would bow;
My heart fulfil its vow.
Some offering bring Thee now. Something for Thee."

This hymn, Tom MacDonald's favourite, was sung often at the Club and became a symbol of the essential spirit of Inverness YMCA. The menial service rendered unseen by human eyes (though the results were admired and appreciated) was Wilfred's "something for Thee." His heart was open to God, his life was available for whatever God wanted him to do. Thus it should be no surprise that during one Sunday evening service God challenged Wilfred, now five years converted, to radical Christian service. The sermon title was a question. "Do People In Inverness Know You Are A Christian?" As the speaker developed his theme, the Holy Spirit worked a deep sense of responsibility into Wilf's listening heart.

"Being a postman by this time, I was familiar with each route in the town of Inverness," Wilf said. "I made a plan to cover the whole town with Gospel tracts, a package to every house." Wilfred knew the whole project would entail knocking on the doors of close to ten thousand houses.

The package contained two tracts. One tract, in the form of a bookmark, opened out to display six panels of print. On the first panel were the words, "The seed contained herein is guaranteed to take root and bear fruit in any soil." The second tract, supplied by Victory Tract Club, also laid out the way of salvation very clearly.

When his second morning postal distribution was completed, Wilf set out on a third delivery, systematically covering the whole town in about a month. He remembers one lady recognizing him as her postman and asking him, "Is this a special delivery?"

"It's very special," was Wilf's reply.

As the burden for the spiritual welfare of other people grew, Wilf found innovative ways of spreading God's Word through tracts. On his postal delivery route, he never passed a public telephone kiosk without leaving a number of tracts for whoever may use the phone next. Also, when loading mail to the trains, before passengers were aboard, Wilf took opportunity to distribute tracts throughout the carriages, accompanying each tract with a prayer that God would use it to bless somebody.

While Wilf was learning more and more about the Christian life, the YMCA management committee was sustaining the old tried and true methods of cultivating and sustaining spiritual growth in the lives of the YMCA members. Bible study every Friday evening was the central feature of Club life. Since Mr. J. A. Ferrier had taken over in 1951, the Friday Bible study had prospered spiritually and had been the means of grounding new Christians in the faith. Mr. Ferrier, retired from a civil service position in Jamaica specialized in Scriptural dispensational teaching which described the characteristics of the various chronological eras outlined in the Bible. His classes had the effect of showing the sovereign majesty of God through all the ages and in all the affairs of nations and individuals.

After Mr. Ferrier retired in the late 1950's, his place was taken by George Mackenzie, of Inverness Ebenezer Hall. George was a popular teacher with a practical outlook on life and a burden to help young men become Christians who are useful in the Master's service. George's classes on Romans and the Epistles of Peter were of great help in building up the present writer in the period 1955-1957. Later, George MacKenzie taught a Girls' Bible Class while the boys were taught by Archie Frame from Ebenezer Hall, a highly gifted Bible teacher. Archie Frame headed H.M. Income Tax regional office in Inverness, before moving to Nottingham, then to Glasgow as head of Scotland's Income Tax Department. He was a knowledgeable and polished Bible teacher in demand as Conference Speaker throughout British Assemblies. Archie and his wife Mamie (to whom also the Club owes a great deal) took a great interest in the YMCA and gave of themselves freely for the advancement of the work there.

"I grew rapidly under Mr. Frame's Bible teaching," Wilf was to recognize in later years. "I particularly enjoyed his studies through the Gospel of John. And I remember an evening when Mr. Frame dropped a bombshell. He refused to teach the class any longer unless one of the class members took responsibility to lead it."

Wilf became that person, taking the chair, leading in the opening hymn and prayer, and introducing the speaker each week. Obviously, Archie Frame saw clearly the potential leadership in his class members and determined to encourage it by all means possible. It was a sad day when Archie Frame moved away from Inverness. It was an even sadder day when the YMCA boys, who had benefitted so greatly from his ministry, were informed that Archie Frame had died suddenly in 1986. Perhaps the loss to Inverness YMCA is best shown by sharing the reminiscences of one long-time Club member, Joe MacKenzie, who has served in virtually every Board position during his almost forty-year time at the YMCA.

As a group of young Christians at the YMCA, we found the Friday night Bible Class to be one of the highlights of our week. Studying the Scriptures under the guidance of Archie Frame was indeed a corner stone in building us up in our faith. As well as having a thorough knowledge of the Word, Archie was a natural teacher. His pesonal care and concern for the boys and young men in the class, especially for their spiritual growth, created a loving bond which made us both respect and love him. Of course, this kind of relationship made it easy for us to learn from Archie. Of the twenty or so who regularly attended his class, there are many who still recall that time as a period when they not only learned the fundamentals of the faith but also became grounded in the truth that God's Word was to be lived out in one's daily life. We were influenced not only by Archie's teaching but by the gracious manner of his life.

God chooses men for specific tasks and I have no doubt Archie was raised up for this work, the full fruit of which will be revealed on that Great Day.

I recall very well the spiritual atmosphere of these classes and the keen mind of our teacher as he compared scripture with scripture, unfolding to us the truths which were to impact so deeply our future lives. Subsequently, while sitting under the ministry of other men, I would often discover that I had first seen this truth or that truth at Archie Frame's YMCA Bible class.

The apt illustration, the old truth expressed in a new and original way, the relevant application - all of this, under the sweet influence of the Holy Spirit, left a lasting impression on all present. I recall clearly the old adage from Archie as he encouraged us to search the Scriptures. "Whenever you see a 'therefore' - look to see what it's there for!"

Perhaps the most fruitful aspect of these years of teaching from Archie Frame, and other YMCA teachers, was that we were imbued with the importance of personal Bible Study and the truth of the Apostle Paul's advice to Timothy. "Study to show thyself approved unto God, a workman that needeth not to be ashamed, rightly dividing the Word of truth."(2 Tim.2:15)

Joe MacKenzie's sentiments concerning Archie Frame are echoed by all the YM boys who sat under his ministry.

"In those days, Tom set us up to pray, each one having a prayer partner." Wilfred continued his narrative of YMCA life in the early sixties. "My good friend Dunc Urquhart was my prayer partner. It seems to me now that God used Duncan to help me in so many ways. When we prayed, Duncan had lots to say to the Lord. I dried up after a couple of sentences. 'How do you manage to pray like that?' I asked Duncan. He told me that prayer was simply speaking to our Heavenly Father who was more concerned about what was in our heart than the words we used in prayer."

What Wilfred learned from these prayer sessions was that God's children can come "boldly to the Throne of grace" to obtain mercy and to find help in time of need. Prayer became real and precious as Wilfred recognized the intimacy of true relationship with God, the blessing of being accepted by God through His Son, Jesus Christ. As he learned these things, Wilf's prayer life deepened and broadened to include a particular category of God's servants.

"I started to pray for missionaries," Wilf smiled at the

recollection. "Mrs. Campbell of the Free Church ran a monthly BMMF prayer meeting and wanted somebody to lead. Tom put my name forward. I started it with great trepidation but found it so satisfying and blessed that I actually volunteered to lead the OMF monthly prayer meeting as well."

In conscientous preparation for these monthly prayer meetings, Wilfred read and summarized prayer letters from many missionaries. As he did so, the Lord began to exercise his heart. There was no specific burden. There was a general but acute awareness that these missionaries for whom Wilf prayed were engaged in the most important work a person can do.

Along with prayer, Wilf re-organised his financial expenditures so as to take on partial support of four missionary families. Then there were special projects. One of those involved the purchase of a Land Rover to assist a WEC missionary working in Upper Volta. The vehicle was needed to service the 35 or so villages clustered around the main village of Malba where the Mission central church and medical work was located. Wilf took a leading role in supporting the project personally and encouraging others to do the same. That Land Rover was to feature in Wilf's own life a few short years later.

Other highlights of Wilfred's first years at the Inverness YMCA included summer camping in a big bell tent set up at Loch Dunchelchig with twelve to fifteen YMCA boys; three visits to the historic Keswick Deeper Life Convention in the beautiful Lake District of England; annual attendance at the "Keswick of the North", the Strathpeffer Annual Christian Convention; and helping to organise and conduct follow-up activities for the John Wesley White evangelistic campaigns sponsored by Inverness YMCA. These meetings are worthy of special mention. We back track to the late 1950's to pick up the first contact John Wesley White had with Inverness YMCA.

Mr William J. Anderson and Minie Anderson.

Chapter Sixteen

John Wesley White

In the mid-fifties and on into the early sixties, Inverness YMCA provided great opportunities for service as well as for learning. One of the major benefits to members was the part they played in helping to organise region-wide evangelistic campaigns. Among the most memorable of these were the John Wesley White Crusades of 1955 and 1957.

John Wesley White was a Canadian born in the heart of Saskatchewan's prairies. Saved early in life, John always knew he would be a preacher. He started early, participating in meetings in his early teens. In fact, at age fifteen, he was once billed as "The boy preacher of Canada."

Graduating from Moody Bible Institute in 1948 and Wheaton College in 1952, John found himself in Belfast, Ireland conducting evangelistic tent ministry under the auspices of Youth For Christ International. In Ireland, John met and later married Kathleen, an Irish colleen. He enrolled in Ph.D. studies in England's Oxford University. Intellectually gifted, and unique in oratorical expressions, John was soon sought after as a campaign speaker in the United Kingdom.

In preparation for the first John Wesley White campaign sponsored by Inverness YMCA, club members blanketted the town with Gospel pamphlets which also served as invitations to the meetings. Just about every house in Inverness was reached, and invitations were sent throughout the Highlands. The meetings were well attended with many tokens of spiritual blessing. John Wesley White's messages, powerfully delivered, were couched in terms unfamiliar to Highlanders. The newspapers of the day carried a story of a man in Oban who claimed to be Christ. John's sermon title that evening was, "Is the Messiah in Oban?" A message on Samson was entitled, "A Haircut In The Devil's Barber Shop!"

Though John Wesley White's sermon titles were novel, his message was old-fashioned in the best sense. "Whosoever shall call upon the Name of the Lord shall be saved." "Turn ye, turn ye, for why will ye die?" "He, His own self, bare our sins in His own body on the tree." John believed and preached, without ambiguity, the Gospel which is "the power of God unto salvation to all who believe..." As the campaign progressed, night after night the preacher exalted the Person and Work of the Lord Jesus, His sinless life, His substitutionary death and triumphant resurrection. During the series of meetings God's Word was once again vindicated as souls were drawn to the Saviour in accordance with the promise, "I, if I be lifted up, will draw all men unto me."

When he completed his Ph.D. studies, John Wesley White with Kathleen and their children Bill, Wes, Paul and Randy, took up residence in Toronto from where John conducted a world-wide evangelistic ministry as associate evangelist with The Billy Graham Evangelistic Association. He always remained an esteemed friend of the Inverness YMCA.

At the time of the Inverness campaigns, John had been helpful in advising the three young men who left the Club to go to Winnipeg Bible College. A man of prodigous memory for details, John instantly recognized, thirty years later, one of these three men who happened to meet him at a Billy Graham crusade meeting in Los Angeles, California.

Now conducting an international television ministry out of Toronto and continuing as associate evangelist with Billy Graham, John is fondly remembered in Inverness YMCA for his faithful, earnest Bible-centred preaching and warm interest in the young Christians there. But John remembers Inverness YMCA as giving him something - affirmation that God honours those who honour Him. "I was amazed," John said when interviewed recently (thirty-five years after his first visit to Inverness). "YMCA founder John William's evangelistic and educational intentions were being set aside in most YMCA Clubs across the world. I discovered, to my great surprise, that the YMCA's original mandate was being fulfilled in Inverness."

Under the Board's leadership, Inverness YMCA activities focussed sharply on winning souls to Christ. As already noted, the early fifties were a time of spiritual awareness in Scotland generally, and this awareness continued through the whole decade. For the YM, the period was rich in blessing. The young men whom God gathered around the leaders as the nucleus of the Club shared in the hands-on experience of arranging Gospel Campaigns, Deeper Life Meetings, and Personal Evangelism.

The first YMCA John Wesley White campaign took place in January, 1957. Though it was a Gospel outreach, God's people in the town were challenged by the text printed on the invitation. "What will happen," the pamphlet questioned. "If My people, which are called by My Name, shall humble themselves, and pray, and seek My face, and turn from their wicked ways; then will I hear from heaven and will forgive their sin, and will heal their land. (2 Chronicles 7:14).

Individual church people, regular supporters of God's work at the YM, responded with prayer and zealous efforts to invite unconverted friends to the meetings. The old building on Bank Street groaned under the weight of the crowds and goodly numbers of professed conversions were noted. The event was so blessed that John Wesley White was invited back for another series of meetings in September of the same year. The Sunday Night meeting was held in the Empire Theatre to accommodate the crowds and hopefully attract some who wouldn't enter a church. Once again, the Almighty was pleased to bless the preaching of the Gospel and souls were brought to Christ.

Though fundamentally conservative in both his theology and his preaching, John Wesley White had a habit of finding flamboyant titles to his messages. During that campaign the audience heard a series of messages entitled, I name "The Biggest Liar in Inverness," (the devil); I predict "Man's Ride in a Space Ship," and, I answer "Should a Murderer Die?" People from Macrae and Dick's garage and family members of the YMCA boys who never attended church came to these meetings.

Keith Martin and Alistair MacDonald, 1952.

Chapter Seventeen
Centenary Celebrations

The early 1950's commenced an era of utilizing all means to win some, and the celebration of the YM's centenary gave added impetus to programme activities. Christian films had become relatively popular. A showing of the Bob Pierce movie, "Dead Men On Furlough," on March 1, 1957 introduced another evangelist to the YMCA platform. He was Hugh Walker, an Irishman who emigrated to Canada and now worked with Bob Pierce as an itinerant evangelist. Hugh Walker was invited back in 1959 to help Inverness YMCA celebrate its centenary with yet another extended Gospel Campaign.

The Moody Bible Institute series of Fact and Faith films were also used with benefit, as were the Billy Graham Gospel films.

The YMCA Centenary celebrations included the visit of a team from Winnipeg Bible Institute. Former YMCA member Ed Hughes, accompanied by a Belfast man, Cecil Brown (an excellent preacher and youth worker) and Peter Dyck, soloist, held gospel meetings for two months in Scotland and Ireland. The meetings were arranged by the YMCA and the student team conducted an average of almost three meetings per day (including Open-Air gatherings and House-gatherings).

In the mid-fifties, George Henderson returned to his home town of Inverness after retiring from a 25 year Secretary-ship of the YMCA in Durban, South Africa. Mr. Henderson, who was a prolific and highly popular author (he also wrote under the pseudynom Henry Durbanville) took an interest in the Club. Though over eighty years of age, this excellent Bible teacher presented a series of classes on subjects helpful to

Christian living.

Other YMCA-sponsored speakers of the period included Rev. Calvin Theilman, B.D., of Texas; Welsh evangelist, Rev. W. Myrrdin Lewis; Captain Henry W. Uffelin, a blind preacher and Bible teacher from Jamaica; and Major R. Aldworth, who was also a featured speaker at a special rally connected with the John Moore meetings sponsored by the Inverness Baptist Church.

These ministry efforts, by God's grace, produced abiding fruit. Some of the young people who passed through the Club during those years went on to wider ministries. There were the three lads who went to Winnipeg Bible Institute. It has already been noted that James Scobbie went on to pastoral ministry. The two other lads also continued in ministry. Ed. Hughes worked as a Child Welfare Social Worker before entering full-time pastoral ministry and later Rescue Mission work; and Alister Cameron continued his trade as a baker while serving the Lord faithfully in his home assembly and widening out his ministry to preach and teach at other assemblies in his region of Canada.

There were other young men from this period who entered Christian service - and young women, too. Betty W. Kirsch went to Prairie Bible Institute before embarking upon a twenty-five year missionary career in the remote Aleutian area of Alaska. Another girl, Joan Parkins, served the Lord in Australia before moving to Vancouver, Canada, where she still maintains a ministry of witness to the saving grace and keeping power of the Lord Jesus Christ.

In the early sixties, a man named Dr. McCoy passed through the Club. Dr. McCoy's unique call to ministry when he had passed seventy years of age, and the story of God's Work in and through his life made his visit a blessing.

In 1963, the YMCA brought Gladys Aylward to Inverness. Those who have read The Small Woman will know the story of how this diminutive lady missionary in China led her missionary orphanage children through the mountains to escape maurauding communist soldiers. Her appearance at the YMCA-sponsored meeting in the East Church, drew an overflow audience and her simple message of God's trustworthiness in difficulty affirmed the faith of many. It may also be mentioned that the (now retired) minister of East Parish Church of Scotland, Rev. Donald MacFarlane, helped the YMCA greatly and always proved himself a good friend of the work.

As well as these and other internationally-known speakers, local preachers and teachers also fuelled the spiritual life of Inverness YMCA (and its Gospel outreach). Mr. J. Ferrier lectured on "The Course of Time" (dispensational teaching) and "The Revelation", subjects which the present writer can attest to as being spiritually upbuilding and assuring of the sovereign rule of God in the affairs of this world. Young men who had become attached to the YMCA in that period included David Ireland and George, Leslie and Iain Dunn.

There were also missionary teams from WEC, led by Jock Purves. WEC's motto, (often quoted by Mr. Fran Rowbotham, WEC representative and friend of long-time YMCA president Mr. John MacPherson) came from C. T. Studd's words and read, "If Jesus Christ be God and died for me, then no sacrifice can be too great for me to make for Him." The spirit of that motto was evident in the WEC teams who travelled Scotland conducting Jubilee rallies.

A typical roster of speakers for The Inverness YMCA Friday evening Bible Class of that time reads as follows:

February: Rev. Wm. Campbell (Late of Garrabost)
March: Rev. D. MacDonald (Greyfriars Free Church)
April   Rev. M. Campbell, (Resolis Free Church)
May   Rev. D. Sutherland, (West Parish Church)
June   Rev. J. M. Moore (Inverness Baptist Church)

Speakers expected after the summer two-month break included Rev. D. M. Campbell; Rev. I. Montgomery; Rev. D. MacFarlane; Rev. G. C. Dunnet; Mr. George MacKenzie; and, Mr. A. Naismith. A special note added that in November, Rev. William Still (Aberdeen) and Rev. J. Philip (Edinburgh) would speak.

The fruit of converts from these various YMCA efforts highlighted the need for systematic Bible study to build up the young Christians in their most holy faith. Gradually, the Friday night Bible study became the focal point of teaching. George MacKenzie taught the Women's class. The Men's class was taught by Archie Frame.

It is a tribute to the winsome power of the Bible that such a large group of young people eagerly gathered each Friday evening to sit under the teaching of the Word of God. It is also a tribute to God's servants who "broke the Bread of Life" to these willing hungry souls. George MacKenzie and Archie Frame both taught the Bible systematically and contextually. It was as good as any formal Bible College training - and the results were carried out to the many Inverness churches which were represented by their young people who attended. Only God knows how much the Inverness churches owe to the YMCA Friday night Bible Classes which, along with the Tuesday Class, went on for many years; the Friday class continuing into the present date of writing.

With such rich spiritual fare, it is no wonder that the old Hall on Bank Street hosted crowds again and again. Special missionary events and the Annual General Meetings of various Mission Societies also attracted huge crowds. The Unevangelized Field Mission, for example, had held its AGM in Inverness YMCA for forty years and drew an audience of over three hundred. A problem became evident when the floor of the hall creaked out its resistance to the kind of punishment it was now too old to bear. While people enjoyed God's blessing in the hall, Secretary Tom MacDonald prayed downstairs that the floor would hold. Tom's prayer must have been a prayer of faith as the choice of his prayer venue meant he would have been under it if the floor did give way! The floor did hold; but it was obvious the time was fast approaching when the old building would have to be replaced. The nonexistence of cash for such a project, however, made it easier to delay definite plans - until one night, 350 people crowded into the Bank Street Hall for the 1968 UFM AGM. The potential for tragedy so struck Tom that he determined the moment had come. With characteristic abandon, he immediately announced plans that the old building was to be demolished and a new one in place - and Tom declared it was all to happen in the impossible time frame of eight months!

Margaret and Norman McGrail, 1992.

Members of Invernes YMCA Club who attended the annual general meeting, when five members received medals from the president, Mr M. Mac-pherson, for good service to the club. The five youths (seated) who received the medals are (left to right) — William Jamieson, T. Urquhart, R. Morrison, J. Mackenzie and D. Morrison. Seated on their right is the president, Mr Macpherson, and on the left, vice-president Mr D. Quinn.

Chapter Eighteen

One Man's Faith

Once the decision was taken to demolish the old building and replace it with a new, the Management Committee threw itself into making the dream a reality. The new YMCA, like the old, would be a denominationally-neutral centre which would benefit all churches. With this in mind, Tom called a meeting of the Inverness clergy and prominent Christian leaders. All he asked of them was that they would allow their names to be used as friends who approved the project. He didn't ask for money, just for moral support.

"I think they thought I was crazy," Tom surmised. "When I told them we had no money and we expected God to provide 30,000 pounds (In today's purchasing power, about 229,000 pounds.) only three out of fifteen gave support. One was a minister, the other two Christian laymen. The remaining twelve, mostly ministers, thought the idea was pie in the sky. One had been trying unsuccessfully for four years to raise 1,500 pounds for a project in his own church."

Politely thanking the men for coming, Tom deliberated on his next moves. Following planning permission, he gave a rough sketch of the plans to the architects and took the irrevocable step of hiring the Barnett brothers to begin demolishing. On January 1, 1969, the contractors came to the site. "It can't be done by August 8," they advised Tom. "It must be done. If you don't guarantee it, you don't get the job," was Tom's inflexible reply. Work being scarce, the contractors committed themselves to the completion date of what proved to be their last major building project before retiring.

During the demolition and building process, daily activities were moved yet once more to Mrs. Jenny Martin's premises off Castle Street near the Raining Stairs. YM Sunday meetings continued in a little church hall further along Bank Street just off the Greig Street Bridge.

The MacQueen Memorial Free Presbyterian Congregation met at the YMCA hall for many years, its pastor being Ewen MacQeen, son of the founder. When Andrew Wood, one of the YM lads painted the inside of the little church hall being used in the building interim, the MacQueen Memorial congregation was so delighted they gave the YMCA two beautiful platform tables and a lectern, all made from one oak tree from Lochardil. The MacQueen Memorial congregation has since disbanded (after over forty years of existence) but the oak tables remain as a solid reminder of their appreciation for the YMCA.

When the work on the new building commenced, Tom MacDonald put a small box advertisement in the Inverness Courier to announce the fact and appeal for public support. The advertisement drew minimal response. The Board then fully realized that they were cast upon the Lord, that they had entered a test of faith.

Over the years at the Club, the Management Committee had built up a specialized book store for new Christians and those desiring a deeper reality in their walk before the Lord. They purchased their books from various publishers but chiefly from Mr. and Mrs. Danson-Smith, Edinburgh who, with their daughter Grace and son Theo, visited the Club regularly and became good friends and supporters of Inverness YMCA.

Amongst the book store stock were the Moody Colportage Books, a series of Christian classics. Board members had read them all, including one on George Mueller of Bristol. Though they themselves would never couch it in these terms or make the comparison, the Board was in the kind of circumstances which formed the constant milieu of Mueller's life. As leader at the YM, Tom had not only publicly expressed dependence upon God; he had also gone ahead in faith and commenced operations.

Early results from the box advertisement were not very encouraging. However, donations of one size or another came in. The first was handed to a member by an elderly lady who walked the two miles from Holm Mills into Inverness to deliver what proved to be the smallest donation received. Though followed by others of greater magnitude, that 'widow's mite' was a great encouragement to the Club.

Over at Inverness Royal Northern Infirmary, some Christian nurses decided to have a sale in aid of the YMCA. Miss Low, the matron, kindly gave permission for them to use the recreation hall. Hospital staff did the catering for teas, and, from that first sale, the nurses raised 600 pounds to help with the new building. The event was so successful that thereafter the nurses held it yearly.

Trusting the Lord for wisdom, the Committee also developed a campaign of accessing trust funds, public granting bodies, and government departments with related interests in some of the YMCA programmes.

For the present reader's benefit, it must be restated that the YMCA was a voluntary organisation, led by a Committee of younger Christians with little experience and other, sometimes conflicting, interests. Their committment was unquestionable and impressive, but none of them would have claimed the kind of leadership responsibility which God evidently placed upon Tom MacDonald. His call to serve God at the YMCA was as real and binding as any minister's call to any church, or any missionary's call to any mission field.

Because everybody recognized that final responsibility lay with Tom for what happened at the Club, it was just as widely recognized that Tom's word also constituted final authority for what happened at the Club. Dashes of democracy were

dimly discernible in the discussions between Committee
members at formal meetings. Certainly, Tom evaluated the
opinions offered by others - but when he arrived at final
decisions, they were as irrevokable as the law of gravity.

It was not a question of Tom wanting prominence or power.
Rather, it was a response to the ever-present dangers which
surround a work of God when it is democratized. Many of the
present "Christian" organisations, local YMCA's and even
formerly conservative churches, have so far departed from
Bible standards which formed their founding principles that,
sadly, "Ichabod" (the glory has departed. 1 Sam.4:21) may be
written on their portals. Much of the process of their decline
can be attributed to the fact that God did not find somebody
willing to "stand in the gap" and prevent erosion, somebody
willing to boldly proclaim, "Thus saith the Lord" in the face
of human opinions. Tom was that kind of person, and his
younger colleagues appreciated then - and, many years later,
still appreciate and acknowledge - the "rightness" of Tom's
ministry methods.

Thus, questions about how to finance the new building were,
ipso facto, Tom's responsibility under God. It was in God that
Tom trusted even as he scoured the country for grants and
gifts. And it was God Who, through many human agencies,
provided the required means for the building project.

As well as contacting the Scottish Education Department for
financial help, Tom threw himself into doing the kinds of
things the YMCA did to raise funds every year. The Sale of
Work was an event which brought the whole YMCA constituency together. That year, the Sale of Work brought in the large
amount of around two thousand pounds - a great boost to the
building fund. This amount would have a purchasing power of
around 14,500 pounds today

Meanwhile, on the job site, the contractors pulled one beam
out from under the hall floor - and jumped clear in surprise as

the whole floor collapsed. The floor had been in a far worse state than anybody had thought. If there had been any doubt about the necessity of getting a new building, here was the evidence.

A Courier reporter of the day wrote this of the progress being made. "Little more than the shell of the YMCA building on Bank Street, Inverness, is now left, but, if things go according to plan, it should be replaced in August by a new Hall which would be a real boon to the Inverness Branch of the Association which has occupied the building for more than ten years and which this year will be 110 years old. The new building, the total cost of which is estimated at 30,060 pounds, (about 279,000 pounds in 1992) will have an office, a library, a games-room, a lecture hall which can accommodate a full badminton court when required; two shower-baths which will doubtless be appreciated by the badminton enthusiasts; and a canteen, with wide windows overlooking the river. 5,000 pounds is still required to meet the cost, however, and it is hoped that friends and members will rally to the call - including ex-servicemen who benefited in many ways by the YMCA's efforts during the war."

Going on to describe the history of the old building, the reporter noted that "The building now being demolished on Bank Street has fulfilled many purposes in its day. In 1843, at the height of the Disruption, it was built to accommodate the English Free Church (generally known as the Free High), the forerunner of the present St.Columba High Church on another site at the corner of Fraser Street and Bank Street. It (the old YMCA building) was opened for public worship on Sunday, December 31 (Hogmanay).

By 1850, the church had become too small to accommodate the congregation and the present St. Columba High Church was built. Since then the older building has been used by various organisations as well as the YMCA and in the twenties it became known as the Maud Lawson Memorial Hall for Boy Scouts. Its disappearance in what is hoped will be the march of progress, coincides with that of Queen Mary's House, Bridge Street, which is now almost completely demolished."

The opening of the new YMCA building was celebrated on August 30, 1969. Once again, we utilize the fine reporting of the Inverness Courier to describe the occasion. Headed "New YMCA in Inverness", with a subtitle "30,000 Pounds Building Opened" the article's lead paragraph offered, in non-theological language, an insightful glimpse of the driving force God used to bring the building into being.

"The sheer doggedness and tenacity of the Honorary Secretary of the Young Men's Christian Association, Mr. Tom MacDonald, and many members and friends of the YMCA in relentlessly approaching a multitude of sources for financial help to build a new YMCA building in Bank Street, Inverness, ... saw fruition on Saturday, when over 500 people assembled for the opening ceremony and service of dedication in the recently completed premises."

The article went on to report the contributions to the programme of various dignitaries, including Inverness Provost, W. A. Smith; Miss Elizabeth Rose of Kilvarock, (Chief of the Rose Clan); Rev. William Still of Aberdeen; Rev. W. R. MacKay, hospital chaplain; Mr. A. Frame, YMCA honorary president; George Smith, General Secretary of Scottish Council of YMCA's; and, Rev. W. Johnstone, Scottish Secretary of Unevangelized Fields Mission. A telegram from Balmoral Castle was also read, as follows: "Please convey to all the members of the Inverness Young Men's Christian Association assembled on the opening of the new building on their 110th anniversary, the sincere thanks of the Queen for their kind and loyal message of greetings which Her Majesty greatly appreciates."

Although Tom characteristically spurned personal recognition, no less a person than Rev. William Still, in no less a manner than while addressing the Almighty in prayer, acknowledged Tom. In his prayer of dedication for the new YMCA building Rev. Still thanked the Lord for those people of a past generation who, under God, brought the Inverness YMCA into existence, Rev. Still then gave expression to the sentiments of everybody who knew Tom when he fervently prayed, "...Especially, O Lord, do we thank Thee for Thy dear servant here, and each one of us, even those who have devoted themselves for many a few years to the service of Thy cause here on this site would acknowledge that it's largely by the inspiration and the vision and the drive and the holy passion and compassion of our beloved Tom that this work has continued." Rev. Still went on to thank God for the "many fine young men in whose eyes we have seen the light of Christ," young lives that have been converted and led out into Christian service through the instrumentality of the Club.

Tom closed the formal part of the Dedication and Opening meeting by giving thanks to all those who had taken the time and interest to attend. The Courier Reporter recorded that "the honorary secretary, Mr. Tom MacDonald ... said that too much credit had fallen upon himself when in fact everything had been done through team effort. Mr. MacDonald said that the building would not have been possible without the help of the Education Authorities and generous grants from the Highlands and Islands Development Board. He commended the Ladies' Committee for the long hours of work they had put in and thanked the various churches in the town for the use of their halls during the rebuilding programme.

Turning to face Provost Smith, Mr. MacDonald said, with a smile on his face, "We have been able to pay for our building. We have opened the building itself without any debt - but we still need quite a lot of money." Provost Smith took the ribbing in good spirit and said he would take note. In a more serious vein, Mr. MacDonald told those assembled that the building was one thing, but furnishings and equipment was another matter. He said the building was empty and they had found it necessary to borrow chairs for the audience to sit on during the opening ceremony. "If we had the money to get gymnastic equipment, we could offer more to the youth of Inverness. We appeal to Invernessians to help us. There is no kitchen equipment, there is no linoleum on the games-room floor ... I could go on and on. You are the only people to whom we can appeal."

Continuing his expression of thanks, Tom named the churches which had helped by making their halls available during the building interruption. They were the East church, the West church, the Salvation Army, the Free North church, and Greyfriars church.

Tom also made special mention of two brothers, David and John Lee, who provided carpets and upholstered furnishings at cost price for the new club. Both David and John served on the YMCA committee, David having filled the office of President.

Notice was also made of a contribution of material from William Pringle, Holm Woolen Mills, and the good work done by Norma MacKenzie and Isabel Morrison in making the beautiful curtains which graced the hall that day. Mr. Finlay MacDonald, Holm Mills, was thanked for storing all the YMCA furniture free of charge and for helping with various jobs around the building site. The formal meeting was then drawn to a close with the singing of Psalm 121. God was honoured and acknowledged through the singing of this psalm which proclaims, "I to the Hills will lift mine eyes, From whence doth come mine aid? My safety cometh from the Lord, Who heaven and earth hath made."

Following the programme a retirement offering basket (actually, two large wastepaper baskets) gave people the opportunity to donate as they made their way downstairs for refreshments and fellowship. The offering that day amounted to 790 pounds. This sum would have a purchasing value of 5785 pounds in 1992.

The upstairs Hall in which the opening ceremony took place that day was named for the Anderson family in particular appreciation of William and Minnie. Both had steadfastly supported the YM through the previous four or five decades and helped significantly during the new building process. The Andersons were very generous in sharing not only their means but also their time and energy to prosper God's work in the YM. The Hall stands as a tribute to their faithfulness, a memorial to their Christian ministry.

The tape recording of that afternoon's joyous celebration reveals something of the way the YMCA support constituency (500 strong that day) viewed the Club's honorary secretary. The Provost's opening speech was interrupted by spontaneous applause at the first mention of Tom MacDonald's name; and later, Tom's call to the platform was greeted with what can only be described as thunderous and prolonged applause. This honest unsolicited recognition, along with Rev. Still's reference in prayer, speaks eloquently of the love and esteem in which Tom MacDonald was held by those who knew him and his work for the Lord. Evidently, the congregation recognized that the new YMCA building was, in some sense, a tangible tribute to the faithfulness, diligence, and zeal of God's servants.

Years later, the writer found in Tom's scrap-book a poem which had become one of his favourites. The poem is a prayer - a prayer which seems to express the texture of Tom's life. The source of the poem is not known but its words have been a blessing, not only to Tom but to many of the young Christians who were being spiritually nurtured through the ministries of Inverness YMCA and the indefatigable efforts of its honorary secretary. All who knew him, and especially those who were the recipients of his sacrificial ministry, will sense the tenor of Tom's life in this poem.

Thought For The Day.

This day is mine to mar or make
God keep me strong and true
Let me no erring bypath take
No doubtful action do

Grant me, when with the setting sun
This fleeting day shall end
I may rejoice o'er something done;
Be richer by a friend

Let there be something true and fine
When night slips down, to tell;
That I have lived this day of mine
Not selfishly, but well.

Group of Members, 1957.

Chapter Nineteen

David Forbes

Progressive parts of Wilf Urquhart's story have been told in detail and we will return to it in later chapters. But Wilfred has been selected as a somewhat typical example of God's abiding work in the lives of many young man who have passed through Inverness YMCA on their way to life ministries. W. R. Mackay is the first on record, but not the first in fact, to do so. Since W. R. Mackay, the long list has included many young men. One such man is David Forbes.

In response to a request for a personal account of how the Inverness YMCA impacted his life, David wrote the following.

"I've been a missionary now for nine years. In preparing me for that, God used Inverness YMCA.

God orders our circumstances. My family belonged to a small independent church which eventually used the lounge at the YMCA for its Sunday services. There I was grounded in an accurate, but not intellectual, theology. Our pastor was the warm-hearted Ewen MacQueen. He loved the Lord. That was expressed most clearly, not in what was said but how he said it. But in any small and independent church a danger lies - of being too insular, too unaware of God at work elsewhere. That is where the YMCA After Church Rally was strategic.

Each Sunday at 8 pm, after our own evening services we'd join the many young men and other YMCA supporters to hear an address. How wonderful it was to be there. I can still remember speakers I heard as a child - General Frost; Professor John Murray on the night he had to stop early due to fatigue. (Professor John Murray, originally from Bonar Bridge, became Professor of Systematic Theology at Westminster Theological Seminary, Philadelphia.)

I remember being handed those small red books of Alexander's Hymns and sitting in a position so as to avoid having the speaker obscured by the pillars in the big hall. The leader and speaker would climb the steps behind the pink and blue pulpit. "Not normal colours for a pulpit," I thought.

It was always cosy in there, even on cold winter nights. People seemed to come into the hall like little flocks of sheep; four men in a row this side; five young ladies on the other; a family of five. The boards creaked as they came and so we boys loved to look round to see who it was. And to us, they were usually late. You see, we just moved from the wee room to the big room. Others had to come down from the Baptist Church on Castle Street, across the Greig Street footbridge from the East Church or up the street from the Free Churches. A blend, a mixture of God's people. Old and young. None of the evangelical churches clung on to their young people in those days. The fashion of Sunday night youth fellowships hadn't begun. It was creeping from the South. but we still had a few years before churches became desperate to totally monopolise the input into their young people. Until that happened, those Highland churches were unique. There was a friendliness amongst God's people; an awarenessof each other. There were no baptist/presbyterian debates. I never heard the proud statement,'Oh, but in our church we....' You hear it all the time now. No, the town was flooded with Reformed Theology. It was devotional, outward looking, and full of grace.

But quite often we weren't the first into the big hall. We were last! Mr. MacQueen, like any man whose heart has more in it than his words could express, repeated himself. He repeated his main points, then his minor points. And, still feeling inadequate, he did so again. It was eight o'clock already. We boys heard the first footsteps coming up the stairs. We knew "the YM boys", as my Dad called them, would need our chairs for the big hall. In those days there was no glass panel in the door into that lounge. So Mr. MacQueen couldn't see the stream of folk arriving. I think I know why the architect put glass in that door when the new building came up!

Of course, we boys saw what was happening long before eight o'clock. If you were at the front of the lounge you could look out the small window. It made the YMCA walls look so thick. But all you could see from that window were the arrivals and departures from the RC church and a bingo hall across the river. Often I've watched cars parking on that side and wondered just how difficult it is to park a car. For a better view across the river, the window nearer the back was vital. And out that window we could just see some of those clean-cut YMCA boys getting on to the footbridge from the other side and making their way to the After Church Rally. I wondered where we'd sit if we got out too late. Being at the front of the big hall meant you couldn't watch people come in late. But we'd be sure of getting a seat - since we were already sitting on the chairs needed for the big hall.

Then the meeting would start. Tom MacDonald would often lead. He had a deep voice, always audible. I wondered if he practised speaking like that. Others, like the Lee brothers or Norman McGrail might lead, or Joe Mackenzie. But it was more interesting when one of "the boys" had to lead - Andrew, Wilf, George, Donald, Calum - they looked awfully tidy. They stopped at the bottom of the platform and let the speaker up first.

I especially loved the singing of the psalms in the YMCA. The hymns were good, too - especially for our congregation where psalm-singing was all we had. We gladly sang the hymns. But the young men at the YMCA could really sing the psalms. It is possibly my favourite sound on earth - those many, young, male voices giving the last three stanzas of psalm 72 the rendering they deserved. "His Name forever shall endure... ."(v17)

But what was most significant in preparing me for the mission field were the talks themselves. Week after week we'd hear firsthand from missionaries recently returned from Africa, Asia or South America. God's kingdom extended beyond Inverness. He was saving people in far-away cities and jungles. And He sent some of His servants there. It was a rare education. We, supposedly parochial Highlanders, delighted to hear that God was working throughout the earth. It fitted perfectly with our theology. If He is Sovereign, then He is Lord of all His creation. We know it - and the stories we heard just proved the point.

I remember going home from the YMCA one Sunday night. I was young enough to be sitting on my Mother's knee as Dad drove to the farm. It must have been winter since Mother had her fur coat on. That night, the missionary had talked of jungles and hard work, of faith and perseverance. I can still hear myself saying to Mum, 'I'd like to be a missionary.'"

Chapter Twenty

Wilfred Urquhart's Call

When David Forbes was challenged to missionary service through the preaching at the Inverness YMCA he was joining a long line of other Christians who had experienced the same call. Some years before a missionary labouring in Upper Volta used part of his furlough to speak at an Inverness YMCA meeting. It was a bit embarrassing for the local leaders that only about six other people attended the meeting along with Wilfred and the ubiquitous secretary. Nonetheless, God was present in a special way and Wilfred left that meeting knowing he was called to full-time foreign missionary service.

Also that night, the collection was put towards the purchase of a Land Rover and Wilfred himself was led to give generously to the project. This led to Wilfred taking a practical interest in God's Work being done through Worldwide Evangelization Crusade (WEC) in Upper Volta. A decade was to pass before Wilfred actually entered missionary service. But the start was made in that meeting so poorly attended, yet so richly blessed. God called! And Wilfred said "Yes, Lord!" - the only appropriate response to the One Who had so graciously reached down into Wilfred's sorrow-filled life and given him the joy of salvation.

From 1960 to 1967 Wilfred served as Assistant Secretary at the YMCA, helping to arrange meetings and generally sharing the burden of leadership. In that period, some of the boys who formed the nucleus of the Club were Harry Chambers, David Murray, Donald Reid, Colin Pearson, Arthur Wood and his younger brother, Andrew. Donald Graham and his brother John Graham also joined the club about this time. Amongst the younger members, David MacEwen was very active.

Donald Graham went to WEC for Bible training then into ministry; Arthur went to Canada to attend Bible School; while young Andrew, a wholly-dedicated member, was being groomed to take Wilfred's place as Associate Secretary. Dunc Urquhart, Joe MacKenzie, Derek Morrison and John MacKenzie were still active, serving on the Board.

During those years, a man called Jack Robertson spoke at a meeting in the YMCA. Wilfred remembers how the Lord used that meeting to speak clearly to him. "I felt sure that I was being called to Upper Volta."

Still, Wilfred remained at Inverness YMCA, serving the Lord wholeheartedly but not yet discerning the next step he should take. On two occasions a team of WEC Bible school students, missionary candidates, passed through Inverness and spoke at the YMCA. "I could see that they were doing what I wanted to do," Wilf admitted. It wasn't long until the next step became clear. In 1967, Wilfred enrolled in the two-year course at WEC Missionary Training Centre.

In following the Lord's leading to attend WEC Centre, Wilfred was voluntarily surrendering the financial security and opportunities for career advancement offered by the Post Office. While he was in college, however, the bonds with Inverness YMCA were maintained and strengthened as members held Wilfred up in prayer and gave money gifts to help him through College. Also, during holiday times, Wilfred returned to Inverness where he had opportunities to preach at the YMCA Sunday After Church Rally and at the mid-week Bible studies.

"Tom himself took a major interest in my training," Wilfred shared. "He helped me financially and was always available as a friend. He made sure I got meetings at the YMCA and that I had everything I needed."

Graduating in 1969, Wilfred knew he would have to learn the

French language if he was to serve God in Upper Volta. He applied to serve with Operation Mobilization for summer ministry in Belgium. He returned to the United Kingdom in Fall and took a Wycliffe Bible Translators' seven week linguistic course.

"Then I went to France to perfect my French," Wilf advised. "I worked in a wee protestant evangelical church in Lens for about a year. I loved it and may have settled there, except a WEC leader wrote and asked what had happened to the call God gave me to serve in Upper Volta." Jolted into a realization that God's call came before personal preference even in the Lord's work, Wilfred returned to Britain.

Before following Wilfred's career further, we will return to Inverness YMCA to pick up the narrative of that institution's progress.

Three Inverness YMCA members are off to Winnipeg. They are Edward Hughes, 32 Carse Road, Inverness; James Scobbie, Cullochy Locks, Invergarry; and Alistair Cameron, 16 Cameron Road, Inverness. All three are twenty-one years of age. They intend to become evangelists, studying at a Bible college in Winnipeg.

Last night they were each presented with a travelling bag and a wallet of notes by Inverness YMCA members, the presentation being made by Mrs J. Martin.

Seen admiring the gifts are (left to right) Mr John Macpherson, president of Inverness YMCA; Messrs Hughes, Scobbie and Cameron and Mrs Martin.

Messrs Hughes and Scobbie leave Inverness to-night on the first stage of their journey. Mr Cameron will follow.

*The Forbes Brothers from Farr. Back row — Alistair, David.
Front row — Ian William Farquhar.*

Chapter Twenty-One

Andrew Wood's Home-Call

Tom MacDonald, now a Managing Director in the firm for which he had worked for over thirty years, was still using all his free time to serve the members and protect the interests of the YMCA. He was being ably assisted by Andrew Wood who started attending the YMCA Games room when he was thirteen years old. Later converted, Andrew became a bright and sensible Christian, in some ways greatly advanced spiritually for such a young man.

Two other young men who were Andrew's contemporaries, Donald and John Graham, were converted in the Club at that time. John, the older, is now an accountant in Orkney and is actively involved in Church work there. Donald is in business in Kentucky, USA, after working with WEC in France.

By the time he was twenty-two, Andrew, who had modelled his managerial style after Tom, took charge of the Club's daily supervision. The boys who used the sports facilities clustered around Andrew, whose popularity helped him lead the boys to YMCA Bible studies and Sunday meetings. Slightly built and not many years older than the boys themselves, Andrew took over where Wilfred had left off. He was at the Club every evening, making sure everything was in order, supervising the general activities and doing all with both firmness and a congenial regard for the boys there.

One day, after being at the swimming baths, Andrew was returning to the Club to take part in a special farewell to Donald Graham, another YMCA member who was leaving that day to attend Bible School. Without warning, a Transit van started up and drove across Andrew's path. Thrown from his motor cycle by the collision, Andrew died in hospital soon after as a result of a broken rib piercing his heart.

Andrew's sudden death was an immeasurable loss to his family and to his second family of brothers in Christ. Dazed and heartbroken, the YMCA boys somehow lived through the next few days, unable to believe that Andrew was gone even as they woefully planned for their part in his funeral service. Tom MacDonald, not only bereft of a loved friend, also had to revert to full leadership responsibility. The Committee's grief was borne in private as they arranged for a grave headstone which would bear sentiments showing the great love and esteem in which Andrew had been held by his fellow-Christians. (This was the second such tribute. Over a hundred years before, Inverness YMCA had erected a similar memorial stone to honour a member named Hugh Cameron, aged 24, who died in the late 1850's and is interred at Boleskine.)

Andrew was buried from the YMCA hall. His funeral service was conducted by Rev. William Still of Gilcomston South Church of Scotland, Aberdeen, of whom more will be said later. Rev. Still, a great friend of Inverness YMCA, preached from the text, "Why this waste?" (Mark 14:4)

Andrew's death was a time of unspeakable sorrow. Yet, in spite of the anguished questioning torn from crushed hearts, all of the boys knew that Andrew was ready to die. Only a week earlier, while participating in an open air meeting at Strathpeffer, Andrew talked about his own readiness to die. Like the apostle Paul, Andrew knew that "to be absent from the body" was "to be present with the Lord." (II Cor.5:6-8) His message that day contained such a prophetic tone in light of his death so soon after preaching it, that Norman McGrail published Andrew's sermon in tract form. Part of the message, entitled This Young Man Said, is copied verbatim from a tape recording made by the Reverend John Macleod, Free Church Evangelist. It is reproduced below.

This Young Man Said .. "Good Evening" (...to the crowd gathered in Strathpeffer village square, Ross-shire, Scotland, on Saturday, September 25th, 1971. Some were making their way to the dance hall across the road. Some were merely passing by. Some were with Andrew for the annual youth weekend of Christian convention. Some listened as he continued...)

"I'd like to say a few words in particular to those who are making their way to the dance hall, or to anyone who is just passing...

I'd like a minute or two of your time...

I'd like to ask you a question tonight. Although this is meant to be my testimony - I have nothing really to offer you but Christ. And I can but ask you to ask yourself one or two important questions tonight.

I'd like you to consider how long you will be alive on this earth - at best you can expect seventy years - And the way some of these people drive about here, you can't even be sure of that.

I'd like you all to ask yourself, 'What will happen to you after death?' You go about from day to day. You seem quite forgetful that some day there will be a judgment. You have to face Jesus Christ, to be judged for your actions on this earth.

What will your reply be? Will He even know you? I can but ask you to consider this. Now there are many reasons, many loopholes. You may come up with a multitude of answers. Of questions as to why you shouldn't even consider your own way. One of these is, 'Look at these Christians.' You know something about him. You know something about her. This hardly the sort of life. You can't be asking me to follow this! We certainly can't. I can but give you an example.

I take a copy of a picture. I ask you to copy it. I doubt if your copy would bear any resemblance to the original. So it is with Christ. We must ask you to set your eyes on Him and Him alone. He is our Saviour. He can be yours too. I would implore you to ask yourself the question, 'What will be your position in eternity?' Ask it this night. Thank you.

(And only seven days later this young man died as a result of a road accident. ANDREW AITKEN WOOD was just 22. An Inverness YMCA leader, keen athlete, dependable, quiet and completely dedicated. In human terms he had so much to live for - a fine young man. But God in His mysterious way had finished the preparation for his eternal service. The Apostle John records '...that His servants shall serve Him.' (Revelation 22v3).

Do you think Andrew sensed something of the coming events in time ... and eternity? Will you give him just two more minutes of your time and read his words again?

Jesus said ..." He that heareth My word and believeth on Him that sent Me, hath everlasting life and shall not come into condemnation; but is passed from death unto life." (John 5:24)

The tract ends with a question. How long - or short - is your life?

In light of the fact that life on earth is our day of opportunity to respond in faith to God's grace and mercy in Jesus Christ, this question is as universally relevant today as it was when asked by Andrew Wood one week before his death.

Tom MacDonald had been secretary for 23 years when God called Andrew home so unexpectedly. Always aware that God's work at Inverness YMCA was and is bigger than any individual, the Board threw themselves afresh into the ministry which called for so much self-sacrifice. In the providence of God, there were other young men in the Club who had risen through the ranks and demonstrated consistent Christian life and willingness to serve God by serving others. Norman McGrail, George Maclean, Colin Pearson, Graham Heard, David Murray, Billy Mackenzie and Calum Sutherland were among those who had come into the Club in recent years. Joining John MacKenzie, David Lee, Joe MacKenzie, Derek Morrison, Harry Chambers, and Tom himself, these newer members rose to the challenge of the hour. Duties formerly cared for by Andrew were shared amongst the members, and everybody did their part. It is impossible to describe the contributions of each one. Sufficient to note the present whereabouts of those who have moved on to other ministries and to present a brief profile of those members of that period who are still actively involved in Inverness YMCA at this time of writing.

Andrew Wood.

Calum and Eileen Sutherland.

Ali Paul.

Graham Heard.

Chapter Twenty-Two

Labourers Together For Christ

Norman McGrail came to Inverness to work with the High-land Development Board. Being married, Norman brought a level of maturity to the group of younger men. He participated in as many Club activities as he could and helped with the worship and teaching meetings until he left Inverness to take a position as representative for StrathClyde in the European Commission centred at Brussels, Belgium. During his time at Inverness, Norman also completed a term as YMCA president.

In response to a request, Norman and his wife Margaret kindly penned the following lines in reminiscence of his days at Inverness YMCA.

We spent twelve years in Inverness before moving to live in Bruxelles, from 1979, during which time many lasting impressions were made. The most outstanding reflection is one of thanksgiving to God for experiences granted in His Providence through different activities in the life of Inverness YMCA. The regular Christian fellowship we found there, flowing freely through all age groups and amongst evangelical believers taught in Biblical truth, has been comparatively rare in our experience.

Many spiritual and practical activities must surely place Inverness high on a worldwide YMCA scale, at least when seen by human measurement. These activities took many forms including the vision to build the much enlarged hall and other modern facilities, combined with the practical enthusiasm and dedication associated with popular sales to raise funds.

*The many rallies held during each year by missionary
societies and others found a welcome 'home' in the YM and
provided opportunities to meet across denominational barriers thus adding to spiritual stability not least in young lives.*

*Summer camps, weekends at Strathpeffer convention or in
the granary at Kilravock castle gave more opportunities to
study the Word of God together and at the same time to enjoy
fellowship and fun.*

*The Hogmanay gathering held regularly on 31st December
was a special event in the YM calendar and formed an
important and colourful piece in the YM jig-saw puzzle.*

*The life of the YM was strengthened and enriched through
the unique leadership of Tom MacDonald whose tireless effort
and spiritual sensitivity needs to be acknowledged in a faithful
record of these years. Tom's fierce defence of the YM and his
support of all who were connected with it in joy or in sorrow
is a hallmark of the man. The 70's was a period when his
leadership from 'the Front' was slowly moved to a group of
younger hands with acceptance and support from Tom himself.*

*In closing these few comments we would like to record one
strong continental connection that has grown from that very
special weekly after-church gathering in the room overlooking the river Ness. Young people and older ones too, from
different churches were brought together for a devotional
meeting and fellowship there even before some churches took
action to meet a need for the activity in the lives of young folk.
We have already noted that bringing together all age groups
in such a warm spirit of fellowship is rarely to be found. The
spirit of the YM was to be found there.*

*One Lord's Day evening we met two Dutch lads, Egbert
Moolenaar and Jan MacDaniel, who were camping in the
Bught Park and who were leaving the next day. They had no
difficulty at all with language. But in order to decide which*

church to attend in the morning they simply looked for church-going young people most like there own congregations in the Netherlands, and decided to go to the Free North. One of them left his umbrella behind in the church and so they returned there to collect it at the evening service. Afterwards, they saw the YM open and came to the after-church meeting. Over a cup of tea we talked and exchanged addresses with no idea that in little over a year we would be meeting them on this side of the Channel.

We next met in the Netherlands when they spontaneously took us on a sight-seeing day trip to the Overflakkee region. Since then, we have visited each other at home on several occasions. A deep and lasting friendship therefore began in the YM. They are fine Christian young men now qualified lawyers and we were delighted to be present at their weddings. Jan still shows us a copy of the Psalmody given to him by Charlie Mackintosh when he expressed an interest in the metrical version of the Psalms.

The Inverness YM has touched lives from other countries as this small incident of an umbrella shows. We gratefully acknowledge it to be all part of the YM Mosaic in our experience. Clearly and wonderfully, there are very many more who can blend their countless experiences of having been brought together and to God there, over the years, in the marvellous Providence of God Himself.

Margaret and Norman McGrail. Bruxelles, October, 1992.

Graham Heard served as YMCA secretary and is now an engineer in Wales, where he is also very involved in local church work; his experience at the YM provides a window through which we may see the richness of God's Work there. Graham writes:

"I came to work in Inverness on June 6, 1970 and attended the YMCA After Church Rally that same weekend. The first

person I met was Tom MacDonald and we went into the meeting together.

That Sunday night was my first encounter with the singing of Psalms unaccompanied and with the preaching of the Word which had its foundations deeply rooted in the Scripture.

My wife joined me from Wales and we found that it was the YMCA, open six nights a week for sports activities, Bible study and prayer, which proved to be a life-line for us, strangers in the area with no family or relatives to visit.

The Friday night Bible studies were a revelation. George MacLean lead some of these and the knowledge and under-standing of theological principles by the youngest of the boys made me wonder what I had ever learned. Here, I heard about a man called 'Calvin'. After the meeting, we older 'boys' often met at Tom's house for a fish supper and to debate Calvin into the small hours of the morning.

It was at the YMCA that Ruth and I met Wilf Urquhart and, later, his wife Pat. Wilf was a missionary in Burkino Faso and Norman McGrail and myself were in charge of the monies collected to support Wilf. Here I was to learn what giving was, something which truly opened my eyes and changed my attitude to giving.

The annual Sale of Work revealed the respect by church and general public when sums of 1,000 pounds and more would be raised; a figure envied even today.

July saw the camp under canvas at Gairloch and since the sun did not set for long at this time of year, the first night was spent playing football, cricket or fishing. Each day began with Bible study and 'hot-dogs'. Times such as these, together with a love for the Lord's work within the YMCA welded us together in a unique relationship which I had not experienced before, nor found since. Hence the awful pain at the tragic death of Andrew Wood in 1971.

The memory of the seven years from 1970 to 1977 which Ruth and I spent in Inverness are precious to us. Chrisann and Sarah were born there; many lasting friendships were formed. God was gracious in allowing me to join in the work of the YMCA, showing me the importance of reaching young men which the established church cannot easily reach. This work is, perhaps, more important today than ever before.

David Murray and Billie MacKenzie, fellow-employees of Boots the Chemists, both helped in Club activities until they left the town. David took a position with a large photographic enterprise in London; Billie Mackenzie is presently pastor of a church in Belgium.

Charles Mackintosh was a schoolboy when he started coming to the Club. Later, he took a prominent part in Committee work before leaving in his early twenties to take the position of Assistant Secretary, Aberdeen YMCA. He now works in a ministry to Chemically Dependent men in Aberdeen.

In the 1980's, before his family came along, Alistair Paul played a very active part in YMCA work. He still lives in Inverness and helps at the Club where possible.

Farquhar Forbes and his brother Alister joined the Board together as noted above. At the time of writing, Farquhar's involvement is curtailled by illness, but his previous contributions were extensive and important. Farquhar introduced supporters of the Club to Deeds of Covenant which, in effect, vastly helped the Club financially. Alister works in Inverness and gives professional advice and help to the YMCA when required.

The following men are still actively involved in Inverness YMCA leadership at the time of writing.

George Maclean

George Maclean grew up in a family which attended the Free North Church. His older brother Norman connected with the

YMCA through using the billiard rooms as a lad. George preferred to go to the Cameron Youth Club to play billiards.

The first time George did venture into the YMCA, as an early teenager, he was met by Wilfred Urquhart who advised him that the Club games room was closed temporarily for repairs made necessary by the vandalism of some rough lads. The next contact George had was when, crossing the Greig Street bridge on his way home from church, he met Harry Chambers coming in the opposite direction.

"I'm on my way to the After Church Rally at the YMCA," Harry told George. "Want to come along?"

Muttering an excuse, George continued on his way home. A year later, after spending a couple of weeks in hospital where he saw others succumb to fatal disease, George became aware of spiritual things. On his release from hospital, he resumed his faithful attendance at Free North church. There, his Bible Class teacher, Mr.Morrison, taught God's Word with fervent conviction. The combination of seeing death close at hand and being confronted with the Word of God Sunday after Sunday opened George's heart. When Harry Chambers met him again on the same bridge under the same circumstances, George was happy to accept Harry's invitation to come to the YMCA rally.

"I don't remember much about the actual service," George reported. "But I do remember catching sight of the cakes and confectionary to be served with tea after the meeting."

No doubt George did justice to the tea and cakes after the service. However, he was far more impressed by the warmth of the fellowship. Welcomed by the other fellows at the YMCA, George began to attend regularly. Soon, he was participating in the camp programme along with Harry, John, John Macleod, Wilf, and some of the other members. George was also invited to accompany the boys on a trip to Glasgow to hear a particular evangelist.

"I'd never been in such an Americanised kind of meeting

before," George recalled. "During the closing prayer which followed the sermon, the preacher said that anybody who wanted to acknowledge their faith in Jesus should lift their heads and look straight at him. I remember looking deep into my own heart and thinking. 'I don't need to look to man. I'm already looking to Jesus, the Author and Finisher of my faith.' That preacher actually did help me inadvertently. He forced me to examine my own response to the Lord Jesus Christ."

George Maclean's new awareness of his own relationship to God, like Abraham's faith of old, soon found expression in works of service. Active in his own church, he also helped greatly in the ongoing work of the YMCA. Though he leads a busy life as High School teacher and author, George continues to serve God as one of the present-day leaders in Inverness YMCA. He co-leads a Friday night youth group, serves on the Board of Management, and has been President.

Colin Pearson

Colin, presently a leader at the Club, provided a brief account of two aspects of his experience of the YMCA when he was a boy. His reminiscence is reproduced below, both for its informational value and also for the insight it gives into Colin's own singular brand of humour.

The twin peaks of the YMCA calendar graced very different parts of the year. The Camp in July was conducted for several years (marvellous to relate) in the sort of West Coast weather which betters the Riviera. After the annus mirabilis of 1976, we returned home almost unrecognised - no Scot could ever be so bronze!

My concern, however, is mainly with the 'YM Party'; this paramount event was held on Hogmanay, and usually extended well into the New Year. We ran it to give young men an option to the typical Scottish New Year celebrations which involved excessive drinking.

In that pre-video age, a major attraction was the presentation of several films. Some attempt was made to cater for all age groups - though if truth were told, mental ages proved flexible at such times.

One particular year, I had the misfortune to act as projectionist. There had been no major calamity during the screening. I relaxed, inwardly praising my own skill as I rewound the hired film. To my horror, pieces of celluloid were spat out of the machine with worrying rapidity. My only consolation in this whole sorry episode was the realization that I had (inadvertently) raised more laughs than the Buster Keaton and Charlie Chaplin we had been watching.

Sport, another indispensable side of the YM triangle, was prominent. We often held the finals of our sports competition as the old year gave way to the new. Do young lads every grow weary? Snooker and Table Tennis seemed to hold even more appeal at 3 a.m.

It would be foolish to deny that we did not overeat. The 'spread' was superb. It would be indiscreet to dwell on any particular faults of youth, but I would dearly like to know what eventually happened to the lad who, unaided, consumed a whole retailer's box of liquorice sticks (ninety-three strips). Medical scientists may also wish to contact him.

Thus far, the social and sporting side of the YMCA's equilateral Triangle has been obvious. But what about the Spiritual. We endeavoured to render the place respectable for Mr. Ewen MacQueen and his congregation who held a service on New Year's morning. A good few of the lads attended the New Year's day service. Mr. MacQeen, - perhaps inspired by the dawn of a new year of grace - certainly had a word for us. His discourse on "By what means shall a young man learn?" remains with me still. I agree it was no easy business to concentrate fully with sleeplessness and inward groanings prominent, but it was a grand way to start a year.

My memories of these times are imprecise and doubtless coloured. However, the fun and innocent excesses of it all is not manufactured. Even as Saint Paul quoted from pagan poets, let me end with words from William Wordsworth which, for me, encapsulate these memories.

"Bliss was it in that dawn to be alive, But to be young was very heaven." (But not quite!)

For the past four years, Colin and George MacLean have conducted a Friday night meeting for young teenage boys. Colin's own two sons, Andrew and Christopher, attend that meeting. Like others in the group (which averages about a dozen in attendance) they are second generation YM members. Colin noted that about half of the boys coming on Friday nights are children of YM members. They all tend to invite their friends from school to the Club, which accounts for the other half. So, there is an element of 'missionary' enterprise involved even at that level.

At the meeting, the boys play energetic games like indoor football - then refuel at the Tuck shop type of Canteen run by the boys themselves. When weather permits, the group has a summer camp. And, of course, the Hogmanay gathering is now an indispensable tradition.

Sandy Finlay

Sandy, now a school teacher, was born in Inverness and belongs to the Free North church. In 1969 he started to attend the YMCA Club activities and is now on the Board of Management.

Sandy's mother, Mrs Findlay (affectionately known as 'Mama' Findlay to many of the boys) supported the Club for many years.

Married to Ruth MacEwen (daughter to William and Dorothy MacEwen) Sandy is very involved in the Club's weekly

activities. A man of keen intellect and possessed of a desire to
see young people come to know God through Jesus Christ,
Sandy is always exploring new ways of ministry. He also uses
his summer vacation time to go camping with the boys, and
has, in the past, been the catalyst in arranging trips abroad for
YM members.

Calum Sutherland

Each person mentioned so far has made his own unique
contribution to the Club, and Calum Sutherland (another
former President and present Board member) is no exception.
Associated with Inverness YMCA since 1967, Calum's states-
man-like poise and considered judgement on Club matters is
highly valued.

Calum lives on the Black Isle where he and his wife, Eileen,
worship at a church in Fortrose. They have two children, Iona
and Scott, both of whom enjoy the twice-yearly Inverness
Association of Church Youth Fellowships' weekend Conference at Kilvarock, the final Rally of which is held at the
Inverness YMCA.

Though his job as quantity surveyor requires Calum to
travel, he makes sure that he is available for YMCA Board of
Management meetings. At the time of writing, he perceives
Inverness YMCA to be going through a period of change
which requires the reshaping of its activities to meet the needs
of a present generation. Reasonably conservative by nature,
Calum nevertheless believes that God has something new for
the YM to do; something which, though it may call for radical
outward changes in programming, will not be inimical to the
YM's historical purpose of bringing young men to Jesus
Christ.

Harry Chambers

Harry Chambers came into the YMCA in 1959. He soon
became actively involved, helping to run the bookstore and

encouraging the younger boys who came to the games room. In July 1, 1959, Harry and Wilfred Urquhart were both welcomed on to the Inverness YMCA Board of Management by then president Mr. John MacPherson. Thereafter, Harry has not only helped in the administrative work of the Club but has maintained a ministry of personal work as the Lord leads and gives opportunity. Harry is unique in his willingness to come alongside struggling Christians and patiently try to help them towards victory in Christ.

Harry is married to Catherine from Balintore whom he first met when Catherine came into the YMCA bookshop after attending a Missionary meeting. The couple have two children, John and Andrew, now young adults at the time of writing. Harry continues to take an active part in keeping the testimony of Christ in the YMCA. In fact, having spent the years of his Christian life in service to Christ through the Club, Harry, who is also an elder in the West Church of Scotland, may be considered an elder statesman of the Inverness YMCA.

Joe MacKenzie

Joe MacKenzie first heard the Gospel through his Cathedral Sunday School teacher, Miss Ferguson. A student at Bishop Eden School, he was also deeply moved by the old hymn which starts with the words, "There is a green hill far away". But Joe did not comprehend the personal implications of the Gospel in those days.

In 1954, Joe was ill in hospital for some months. Tom MacDonald, with whom Joe had been associated years before in the youth committee of the Scottish Covenant Association, visited him regularly. Thus, when Tom later invited Joe to the Billy Graham meeting, he felt obliged to accept. However, the meeting had no immediate effect on Joe's spiritual life.

Following service in the RAF, Joe returned to Inverness. One day in 1956, while visiting his cousin who was the district nurse in Lochinver, Joe attended a Faith Mission Evangelistic meeting. By God's grace, Joe came into the light of salvation through the finished work of the Lord Jesus Christ. That night he was converted and a few days later he linked up with Inverness YMCA.

"I was swept up into a new life," Joe was to say later. "The Bible Classes accelerated my understanding of my new life as a Christian."

Joe's involvement at the YMCA was reduced (but not broken) by some years of intensive study in pursuit of his diploma in nursing. After graduation, however, he took a position in Craig Dunain Hospital, which allowed him to resume his YM activities. Joe has therefore, in more or less measure, been closely identified with, and active in, the affairs of the Club since his conversion in 1956, helping out in varous capacities. He has been Board of Management member, Treasurer, President; in a word, one of the pillars of the Club's ongoing work.

Chapter Twenty-Three

William MacEwen

Though not presently a committee member, William MacEwen is another person whose present connection with Inverness YMCA goes back over many years, in fact, back to the early 1940's. A chartered accountant, William MacEwen has been a constant behind-the-scenes supporter of Inverness YMCA since he first entered its doors as a young lad.

"As a teenager, I went to the YM on Castle Street for the billiards." Willie's testimony gives yet more evidence of the way God used some of the YM's 'less churchie' programmes to bring boys in. "Then I got called up and was away for some years. In 1948 I came back from studies in Edinburgh and took up with the YM again."

A quiet unassuming person, Willie came into the assurance of salvation in 1955, two years after he married Dorothy Cameron who attended the same church. Together they busied themselves with serving the Lord in the church and at Madras Street Mission.

"We had an interesting experience at Madras Street one year," Willie mentioned. "We invited the neighbourhood children to come for a meeting which would be followed by a party. I left the cakes and goodies there in the afternoon. When I arrived in the evening, they'd all been stolen. The Hall was full of children and I didn't know how I would deal with the situation. God dealt with it His own way - a baker came to the Hall with a load of cakes which he said he was not able to sell. He offered them to me at no cost if I could use them. That was a very direct provision from the Lord."

Willie also remembered a time in the YMCA when Tom MacDonald, just back from a trip south, happily thrust a book into his hands. "I found it in Edinburgh," Tom said. "Knowing your interest in the Psalms, I grabbed it as a gift for you." Checking the title, Willie was amused to see that it contained the word Palms, not Psalms.

Willie has always been a good friend of the YMCA . His support and expertise have been tremendously helpful to the Club over the years. Typically, however, Willie MacEwen plays down his contribution, preferring to point to the efforts of other committee members.

"When the new building was first suggested in 1968, most people thought there was no hope of raising the funds. The project would have been abandoned if it hadn't been for Tom. He tried just about every conceivable funding source, getting help from the Gannachie trust, the Russell foundation and a good few others. Then he and the committee organised a very large Sale of Work. It netted the colossal sum of 2200 pounds." Though Willie didn't mention it, gallons of home-made fruit jam, carefully prepared by Willie in his wife Dorothy's kitchen, helped to make that Sale of Work a success.

Here is a first-hand account of some of Willie's experiences at Inverness YMCA.

"I first became aware of the YM when I was about seven years old as a result of regular visits to our neighbour's house by the president, Mr Masson. He came every week after the Sunday evening service at the YMCA.

A few years later when in the Academy I was introduced to the slower of the two billiard tables in the Castle Street YMCA by a school friend. These were clandestine operations so far as my parents were concerned because the game did not then enjoy the profile it now has.

My close connection with the YM did not begin until the fifties when I was asked to become auditor in the aftermath of the sale of the Castle Street Building and the purchase (followed by the unavoidable sale) of the Palace Hotel.

Ashvale, the hostel in Culduthel Road bought with part of the proceeds from the sale of Castle Street, had been lavishly furnished but was showing heavy losses as a hostel. I recollect the caretaker saying that he was actually saving the YMCA money because, wherever possible, he ironed out creases in the bed sheets without laundering them first, and so got the beds ready for the next occupant.

These were difficult days in the Club due to the compulsory acquisition of the Castle Street property. The Committee invited me to attend their next Annual General Meeting and comment on the losses. In a short span of time the YM had been reduced from what promised to be a well-endowed Association to one in dire poverty.

What the YM lacked in money was more than compensated for by spiritual wellbeing. In these days, when differences of opinion occurred, I would bow to 2 Kings 12:15 ("Moreover, they reckoned not with the men, into whose hand they delivered the money to be bestowed on workmen; for they dealt faithfully.") because I knew that several members of the Committee were devoting their entire earnings, except that which was required for personal necessities, to keep the YM afloat. The position was not unlike that of the early believers whose sacrificial giving is recorded in Acts 4:34ff.

The purchase of the Maud Lawson Memorial Hall was a case of 'needs must'. Over a period of two or three years, however, some of the wooden pillars which supported the roof in the hall became more and more bowlike and finally the hall floor was declared unsafe.

At that time, a building committee was set up comprising a few YM members and representatives from Inverness churches. The initial enthusiasm for the building of a new YM on the site of the Maud Lawson Hall waned quickly and when the final plans and estimates were tabled the Committee pronounced the target unattainable and thereafter ceased to function.

One man had faith. For him, no task was too menial. For a period he used to collect odd discarded cups and crockery for the YM by turning out at 6 a.m., beating the scaffies to the buckets. For this same man, nothing was unattainable. His own efforts were herculean and his ability to motivate others was gargantuan. He himself travelled thousands of miles trying to raise funds. Seeing his example, the small membership which included cabinet makers, carpenters, upholsterers and painters all threw their best efforts into the project. They were ably supported by ladies such as Mrs. Minnie Anderson who, with others who served on the Ladies' Committee, set to with a will and made articles for sales of work. The result was that, after building and completely furnishing the new premises as they now exist, there was only a small shortfall.

What has been, and still is, the benefit of Inverness YMCA? I believe it to be a good meeting ground for Christians of whatever persuasion and in the halcyon days of the fifties, sixties and seventies, it was a place where Church of Scotland, Methodist, Brethren, Free Presbyterian, Baptist, Anglican and Free Church met and were indeed all one in Christ Jesus. Moreover, the influence of the YM has gone far beyond Inverness and has reached three continents outside Europe."

Along with those whose testimonies are recorded above, men whom God had called to be an integral part of the Association, Inverness YMCA was also blessed with a cohort of supporters who were crucially important to the spiritual life of the Club. These individuals were so manifestly filled with the Spirit of God and so singularly used by him in the life of young men in Inverness YMCA that it is right to think of them as a vital part of all that God has done there. Some gave financially to help the Lord's work at the Club. Some came to the meetings faithfully and prayerfully. The MacQueen family from Moy, the Forbes' family, and many other individuals from widely-varying denominational backgrounds attended the meetings regularly and gave financial support to young men leaving the YMCA to attend Bible schools or missionary training centres. These dear friends are too numerous to mention by name, and many would prefer that their consecrated offerings of love and practical good works be known by God alone.

However, two people must be publicly acknowledged if for no other reason than that a historical resume of Inverness YMCA could not be complete without their inclusion. The two are Ella Campbell, an unassuming Inverness Christian, and Rev. William Still, a humble, godly minister serving Gilcomston South Church, Aberdeen.

Billy Mitchell with Members at Camp, 1956.

Edward and Helen Hughes with daughter Ruth and son Paul.

Chapter Twenty-Four
Elsie Bella Campbell
(Ella)

Ella Campbell was born in Struan, Skye, the ninth child of a family of thirteen, one of whom died as an infant. Her parents, John Campbell and Elsie MacKenzie, both had Gaelic but eventually spoke English in the home. However, Ella picked up a good working knowledge of Gaelic in the community where she spent the first ten years of her life.

Ella's father was a shepherd who hired out to earn sufficient money to buy his own croft in Bonar Bridge, which he managed to procure in 1908. Ella was ten years old when the family moved.

Other family members (specifically, Dr. and Mrs. Runcie of Tain and Donald Campbell, Ella's younger brother) remember Mr. Campbell as a kind man, a man of "cast iron principles," a man who worshipped God according to his conscience within the fellowship of the Free Presbyterian Church Every day, Mr. Campbell led the family in Scripture reading, prayer, and the singing of a psalm. His surviving children shared that their father did not have a singing voice, but his position as head of the house demanded that he lead the worship anyway. Though an austere man, toughened in body by the rigours of shepherding and toughened in soul by the challenges of church controversy, Mr. Campbell also had moments of fun with his children. Ella's younger sister, Mrs. Jessie Runcie, recalls that when she was a toddler, her father would playfully chase through the garden after her in sheer fun.

"Father was away from early morning till late at night," Mrs.

Runcie also remembered. "There weren't many neighbour children around but with a family our size we had plenty children to play football and rounders. In winter, we sledged down a hill by our house. We had lots of fun."

Both Mrs. Runcie and Ella's brother Donald remember their mother as "the woman of Proverbs 31." Where father was stern, mother was soft. Not indulgent or manipulable, but of a gentle and loving spirit, Mrs. Campbell could draw close to people in caring ways.

Ella inherited both her father's "iron principle" and her mother's caring warmth. Seemingly not converted at age seventeen (when she attended a "worldly" concert, much to the consternation of other family members) Ella changed in such a way that Mrs. Runcie (who was nine years younger) remembers Ella speaking to her of Bible matters.

A bright girl, Ella could have attended University, but circumstances led her to Inverness where she joined her cousin, Jean Grant, in running the Rodmuire School of Dressmaking. Attaching herself to the Inverness Free Presbyterian Church, she was to become a life-long member. But her spiritual ministry burst out far beyond the confines of the Free Presbyterian Church. In God's providence, He had plans for Ella which made her unique in the annals of Christian ministry. Following the promptings of the Holy Spirit, Ella began to attend a Saturday night meeting at Inverness Baptist Church. She also attended the Sunday After Church Rally at the YMCA around 1938.

In those days, a strong sense of separation marked the Free Presbyterian church and Ella was rebuked more than once for not meeting the church's expectation. None-the-less, God used Ella in a way nobody could have predicted. To highlight the uniqueness of this woman of God, it is necessary to describe her and her life setting.

Ella was over forty at the start of the war. Wearing her hair in an old-fashioned style with her straggly bun crowded under an outdated floppy hat, and clothed in conservative fashions reminiscent of a previous generation, Ella could be fairly described as "quaint." Further, her conversation was never trivial, not geared to the common interests of young people. Ella spoke of her Lord continually, and had a disconcerting way of looking into the eyes of the person to whom she spoke. Yet, anyone who remembers those eyes, remembers a crystal-blue clarity, a depth of love reflected, and a warm gentle twinkle which somehow drew forth trust and honesty from the subject of its gaze.

At first blush, Ella was the very opposite of what we would call today, "A youth worker." But God looks at the heart. And Ella's heart was totally and completely given over to God. She had little of this world's goods, in part because all that came in was passed on to others in one way or another.

When the Second World War started, young Kinloss service-men from all parts of the country and overseas found their way to the Baptist Church Saturday night meeting. Nobody is certain now how it all started, but it is most likely that from the Saturday meeting Ella invited one or more of these service-men to her rooms for tea. Word soon spread and Ella found herself entertaining more and more servicemen, some of whom used Ella's classrooms as their weekend "away from camp" quarters.

Not that there was anything in Ella's premises which a young person would find naturally attractive. The furniture within the high-ceilinged apartment was sparse and antique. A large glass-doored sideboard contained a library of Puritan and Reformed Theology volumes; Manton, Owen, McCheyne, Rutherford, to name only a few. A sofa and soft chair, a curtained-off cot where Ella slept (thus freeing up her bed-room for yet more room to be used by the young servicemen) and a set of straight-backed chairs completed the furnishings.

Large ceiling to floor drapes served to effect black-out regulations. And a wee fire did its best to heat the commodious room.

Yet, from the very start, young men were brought to salvation through the ministry of this unlikely prophetess in these unpretentious premises. A photo album bears mute witness to the hundreds of "boys" who passed through Ella's rooms and gained entrance to Ella's prayers. Many of them became known at Inverness YMCA; Ella used to bring them with her to the Sunday After Church Rally.

Younger readers may not bring to mind that food was scarce and strictly rationed in those days of war. Ella had one ration book which allowed her two ounces of butter a week and small amounts of bread, meat, vegetables, in total hardly sufficient to feed one person. Even tea was rationed.

But Ella was to experience the truth with which God challenged the people of Israel through Jeremiah the prophet. "[Am] I a God at hand," saith the LORD, "and not a God afar off?" Outside of the ministries of her beloved Free Presbyterian church; outside of the assistance of organised programmes set up to help service personnel; far off from any human help, this intrepid saint of God humbly offered her little basket of loaves and fishes to the Lord - and He graciously multiplied her offering so as to feed a constant stream of young men, sometimes as many as twenty, coming at unexpected times, staying through unexpected leaves, always ready to eat but unable to add to the food supply themselves because of rationing.

How the Almighty provided "bread" in the wilderness for this precious servant who was doing His work could be the subject of a book. It is sufficient to cite once instance, typical of many, which shows that Ella understood Who was her only avenue of provision.

One day, having no food in the house, Ella prayed for

something to serve the young men who had visited and stayed overnight. When she opened her front door, Ella found a bag containing potatoes and vegetables already peeled and ready for the pot. Alongside them, hanging over the doorknob was a brace of rabbits - more than sufficient for the day's need.

To sit at Ella's table was to sit in the place of learning. But to focus on the human element of God's wonderful doings is to risk losing sight of the essence of Ella's service to God. It was given to Ella as it is given to few to experience the presence of God in and through her life. She did not see that in herself, though others did. But she was quick to ascribe all the glory to God whenever some of her young men entered into new life and humbly confessed the Lord Jesus Christ as Saviour and King of their lives.

Ella kept no records. But some of the young men saved through Ella's ministry have gone on to enter ministry themselves. Amongst them are Gerald Brown, Jack Green, Campbell Henderson, Roy Godber, Rev. Alan Pringle. Campbell Henderson is in pastoral work in Vancouver, Canada, Alan is a minister in England, Roy teaches school and serves as laypreacher in Ontario, Canada.

Inverness YMCA boys also found Ella's humble home to be a place of blessing and learning. Her door was always open and we never visited Ella but we shared in a season of prayer before saying goodnight. She had a way of so loving those whom God brought into her life that each one of us felt that Ella was "my" special friend. Ella also had a ministry to young women, and matching stories of God's grace enlightening nurses, college students and others are plentiful.

One day in 1948, a nurse who had noticed one of her patients reading his Bible, asked him along to Ella's. The young man's name is David Paterson, a native of Inverness and now nearing retirement as a Free Church minister in Perth. David recounts the impact God made on his life through Ella.

Fond farewell for Inverness teacher Miss Ella Campbell, who has retired after 50 years at Redmure School of Needlework, 33 Academy Street, Inverness. Miss Campbell, whose voluntary work befriending Servicemen in wartime and National Servicemen in post-war years, inspired last night's tribute in the YMCA hall, was presented with gifts and a bouquet. Seated with her are the Rev. Alan Pringle (left) and Mr David Lee. Behind (left to right) the Rev. David Paterson, Mr Jack Green and Mr Gerald Brown.

Chapter Twenty-Five

David Paterson

A Tribute To Ella

"Although I was reading my Bible, I was not converted." David settled into his story. "My mother's father had been a godly Free Church man, but I was in darkness about the Gospel. I had worked as a barman for three years in the notorious Market Inn which, strangely enough, had the effect of putting me off drink. But I loved to dance and had no thought of honouring God in my life.

When I met Ella, I was already under conviction of sin, and had started reading my Bible and going to church. Ella took me to the Saturday night meeting in the Baptist Church where I met a bunch of boys from the YMCA. They befriended me and I went with them to the Annual Strathpeffer Christian Convention. Dr. Fitch was the speaker, and I was converted that night.

Since I worked close to Ella's, I was there for my morning fifteen-minute tea break, one o'clock lunch break, three o'clock break and then back at six. For me as a new Christian, it was like going to Bible College. I believe I learned more theology there than at any subsequent time in my life. We talked Scripture, we studied Scripture, Ella introduced me to the great Christian writers, we prayed together. Ella was about fifty by this time, but I felt very comfortable and blessed in her company.

Some time later, I went to Glasgow College to make up studies for entrance to theological degree studies. After two years, I decided I wasn't ministerial material. I got upset and kind of ran away from myself. Seeing a poster in Glasgow which said, 'Settle down at the other end of the world' I impulsively left for Australia. After I hoboed in the bush there for a while, I met (seemingly by chance) Ron Farquher, the godliest man I've ever talked to. His father, Don, headed the Baptist Mission in Australia. In time, he asked me to pastor a rural two-church charge which I did. I had no training but what Ella gave me, and I had to prepare and preach up to eight sermons a week. I even debated an Anglican and a Roman Catholic priest and the latter couldn't believe that I had no formal theological college training.

After one year in these churches I wondered about what I was doing. I was still 'three-quarters' Free Presbyterian. Then I met Oswald Saunders who asked me to manage a Christian Book Store in Melbourne. I did that for a year before going home."

When David returned home, he took with him his bride whom he met in the church he served. Hazel was a Welshborn girl whose family emigrated to Australia when she was in her mid-teens. Being converted in the church there, Hazel grew into a radiant Christian and a supportive helpmate to David.

"I went to Australia because I was running away from myself," David continued. "Now I was home. I had no job, no house, no money and Hazel was expecting our first child. I found myself still fighting the same battle as when I left. It was a battle against surrending myself to the Lord. Finally one day I cried out, 'Lord, what do you want?' The answer came to me through Exodus.' Go forward.' I knew this meant seven years of study for ministerial training, but my heart was willing.

A strange thing happened at that time. It concerned preaching. My very first 'preaching' was a testimony I shared at Castle Street Saturday Night meeting. Then, in Australia, I preached in the awareness that this was a gift from God. When I decided to attend the Free Church College, a church in Elgin had me come to preach with the idea I may serve as student pastor during my studies. Well, I couldn't preach! At that meeting, I closed my Bible after fifteen minutes and left. God, Who had taken everything else from me, took this also. I went to a hotel in Elgin, lay on the floor of my room, and cried for two hours. God met me there, though. His Word came to me as clearly as if He had spoken audibly. The word was, 'I will make you a fisher of men.'

I did become a student pastor, not in Elgin but in Avnamurchan, Argyle. And, the first time I preached there, a wild boy named Douglas MacMillan was converted. He later became the eminent Professor MacMillan of Free Church College, Edinburgh. God gave me back the gift."

After graduation, David and Hazel have ministered in East Kilbride Free Church for five years, in Brora for five years, and in Perth where, at the time of writing, he has served for twenty-two years.

At a special farewell arranged by the YMCA to mark Ella's completion of fifty years teaching at Rodmure and her retirement to Rogart, David preached a message which epitomized the esteem in which Ella is held by those who know her. Likening Ella to Anna who served the Lord in the temple, David went further. He wrote a twenty-two verse poem in tribute to this grand lady who was now closing the long chapter of front-line ministry given her by God. The poem has been read by Ella's 'boys' (and girls) all over the world.

Ella moved to the family farm in Rogart for the early years of her retirement. As years passed, the encroachment of age reduced Ella's ability to care for herself. She spent her last years in the Free Presbyterian Home on Ness Bank, near the Islands, Inverness. Ella became disoriented from her immediate environment and in the last little while of her life on earth didn't recognize her own sister, Georgie, who also lived in the home. Yet, Ella went from person to person sharing the Word of God and especially the psalms which she knew and loved from the days of her conversion as a teenage girl. Tom MacDonald and other YMCA boys visited Ella regularly. She didn't always know Tom, but she always responded with joy to the Scripture reading, the prayer and the occasional psalm-singing which formed part of the visit.

When Ella was buried at Bonar Bridge, Tom MacDonald and other members were there representing the YMCA and the gratitude of generations of young men who were blessed of God through the ministry of Elsie Bella Campbell.

Chapter Twenty-Six

Rev. William Still

The Rev. William Still was another stalwart supporter of, and minister to, Inverness YMCA. Though located a hundred miles away in the East Coast city of Aberdeen, he exercised a great influence on God's work in the lives of the Inverness YMCA boys.

When he was absent, Mr. Still was affectionately referred to as Willie Still. But, his presence brought forth only the greatest of respect. Then, he was Rev. Still.

Mr. Still's first contact with Inverness YMCA came in 1957 when Tom invited him to come and address some meetings. Speaking on the theme of Justification, Rev. Still was used by God to bring Bible truth to the boys. The friendship formed that night brought into existence the special relationship between this busy city pastor and the Inverness YMCA.

William Still's life was driven by one all-encompassing motivation - a compelling burden to preach and teach the Word of God. A fervent evangelist when he first occupied the pulpit at Gilcomston South Church of Scotland in 1945, Rev. Still's preaching attracted thousands to the church. Soon after, however, he came under the burden to teach "the deep things of God." Gilcomston South congregation began to yield ministry students, missionary candidates, doctors, nurses, scientists, people whose lives were led into virtually every kind of helping profession.

Rev. Still's obedience to the Lord in ministry goals did not go unchallenged by Satan. Not particularly appreciated by some ministerial peers who had abandoned the authority of the Bible for the slippery foundations of liberalism, humanism, existentialism, or some other "ism", Mr Still remained faithful to the Lord and to His Word. But, the strain of opposition made his occasional trips to Inverness a highlight for him as well as for the YMCA boys. In a letter to the present writer, Rev. Still remarks on the spiritual refreshing God gave him through his visits to the Club.

Members of the Club in those years remember with awe the sense of God's presence as Rev. Still opened the Word and laid out the riches therein. A bachelor himself, Rev. Still was able to spend long hours in the lounge, the Bible on his knee, a gleam of joy in his eye as he fed the hungry hearts of young Christians. Some of these converts to Christ still smoked in those days - but not when Rev. Still was around. He would repudiate any attention to himself, but as one of those who experienced God's blessing through him, the present writer remembers the respect bordering on a kind of holy fear which most of the boys felt when with Rev. Still. He was loved because he loved. But all of us were constrained to be on our best behaviour in his presence. No frivolity then. No silly joking, or trivial speech. Yet, the times when Rev. Still visited the Club stand out as high times of blessing from God.

And the visits were reciprocated. It was always a huge delight to be part of a group of YM boys going to Aberdeen for the weekend. If it was a Saturday, we would be met by Mr Still who would take our coats, settle us into comfortable chairs, then look into our faces. His quiet, "How are you?" seemed to carry the sharpness of a dissecting knife as his kind eyes, twinkling under bushy eyebrows, peered into your soul. Thirty years later, one of the boys recalls what it was like.

"Mr. Still was a good friend." The volunteer informant knew Rev. Still well. "He came up to Inverness a number of times in those years. I remember a series of meetings he held at Kilvarock. Afterwards, he made himself available to counsel anyone who wished to talk with him. I was struck by my experience (which others later confirmed as being their experience too) that Mr. Still was able to identify the things that troubled me before I told him. He had a great gift of discernment and a great compassionate interest."

Tom MacDonald especially appreciated Rev. Still's interest in Inverness YMCA. Having gone through a rough time of refocussing on spiritual things in the early years of his own ministry, Rev. Still understood the struggles the Inverness YMCA leaders had to endure in keeping Inverness YMCA centred on the things of God. Tom gave of himself without reserve, but received little in the way of spiritual ministry from others. Sadly, the local churches were just as likely to see Tom as a threat, somebody who may entice their young men into the YMCA. Never mind that every YMCA member was also a member of a church and participated in church activities. Never mind that YMCA members sat under the sound of God's Word, prayed, witnessed to their faith in God's Son, sought the Lord for His Will in their lives. Churches of the day had moved to a sense of self-identity which made them jealous for their young people. With one or two notable exceptions, Tom had to go it alone - a situation with which Rev. Still could and did sympathize.

Few people in Inverness, even those in the Club itself were aware that William Still had quiety supported the work financially for many years. Drawing from a private trust established by himself and a few close ministerial colleagues, Mr. Still unobtrusively provided Inverness YMCA with the significant sum of 150 pounds per annum for a good number of years. Sometimes Rev. Still's donation made the difference between the work closing up or the work going on.

Rev. James Philip of Edinburgh, a colleague of Mr. Still, was another good and helpful friend of Inverness YMCA. Rev. Philip came and preached, bringing rich blessings through the ministry of the Word of God.

Rev. Still and Rev. Philip never received any payment from the Club, which could hardly have paid them anyway in the prevailing financial circumstances. But these two dear friends and servants of the Most High came willingly, paying their own expenses and, as mentioned above, contributing to the ongoing ministry of the Club.

Rev. William Still on his 70th birthday, 1981.

Chapter Twenty-Seven

"Hats Off, Coats Off"

In the years following the erection of the new building, YMCA personnel gradually changed as Tom progressively made room for younger men to assume positions of leadership. But the mandate under which Inverness YMCA operated did not change. A restatement of the YM's reason for being was presented to the Annual General Meeting in 1975. It reminded those present "... of our objectives at all times i.e. to further the work of our Lord Jesus and to seek His glory and that at times of discouragement we should remember that God doesn't reward success or failure, but faithfulness."

At that 1975 meeting, T. J. MacDonald had conferred upon him a YMCA life membership in recognition of his long and faithful service to the Lord through the Club.

The following year, 1976, records the attendance of 22 boys at summer camp. Joe MacKenzie became President, Farquhar Forbes joined the Board, and Honorary Chaplain positions were accorded Rev. William Still and Rev. James Philip.

At a special Board meeting in 1977, a matter came up which resulted in Inverness YMCA clarifying and restating its status as an independent YMCA (the only one in Scotland). The issue had to do with new national constitutional amendments dealing with disposal of YMCA-owned properties if dissolution occurred. The response of Inverness YMCA to the proposed amendments is best related by quoting from a letter sent by the Club to the Scottish National Council of YMCA's, which read in part:

"...The Council will have noticed that we have not paid affiliation annual capitation fees for some years now. It should

also be noted that we do not intend to do so in the future. This has arisen as a result of the unanimous wish of all full time members not to be represented on Council.

In Inverness we continue to enjoy fellowship with YMCA members from all parts of the world, and trust this will increase. We are experiencing good attendance at mid-week prayer meetings, Bible studies and the Sunday After Church Rallies. We look forward to welcoming you and Council members at any time."

This amiable separation maintained the status of Inverness YMCA as a completely independent Association which had been funded, built, and operated by local people since its inception a hundred and eighteen years before.

At that same meeting, newly-elected President David Lee acknowledged both the history and the potential of the organisation's work, ending his address with the rallying cry, "Hats off to the past, coats off to the future."

The YMCA was fortunate to acquire the house next door to the new building. The added facility has proven most valuable to the Club. Its acquisition was again an evident blessing from God.

The owner, Inverness solicitor Robin MacEwan, was a good friend of the YMCA. He offered the house to the Club at a much reduced price. However, the Club didn't have accumulated monies to draw upon.

At about the same sime, another life-long friend of Inverness YMCA from Argyle Street, had passed on, leaving five thousand pounds to the Association. This money was made over to the work and, along with grants and donations (plus much hard work by Tom Macdonald and the Ladies' Committee) enabled the YMCA to purchase, renovate, and join the house to the main building.

The total cost of this project was approximately twenty thousand pounds. Everything was paid for in full before completion - yet another manifestation of God's great faithfulness.

As the future began to unfold, much of it had an uncanny resemblance to the past. There was and is the daily care of the premises, requiring good stewardship planning and many hours of Board discussion. There was and is the perceived need of bold new programmes to draw young men into the Club and thus under the sound of the Gospel. There was and is the continual emphasis on world missions, highlighted by the consecration of a considerable portion of the annual budget to regular support for Wilf and Pat Urquhart in Upper Volta; David Forbes, working as an accountant and living as a Christian in a vastly under-evangelized land which forbids proselytizing under pain of deportation and thus must remain unnamed; and Denis and Rivi Mackay in their ministry of Jewish Evangelism.

There has been sadness, too. The minutes of May 28, 1987 which records the call to higher service of Mr. William Anderson also notes the sudden tragic death of Denis Mackay. Denis was laid to rest in a cemetery on the slopes of Mount Olivet in Jerusalem. His wife, Rivi, persevered in their ministry, establishing a Centre for Jewish Evangelism in Tiberias. Inverness YMCA continued to support this work.

Through the eighties and into the early nineties, promising young men came and went as God called them on to further studies or work in other parts of the land. The nucleus remained, however, seeking to carry the torch of Truth and, in due time, to hand it on to others willing to commit themselves to the work.

The majority of these leaders who have served from the 1980's came to the Club as young boys, but are now married men who are raising families and pursuing career goals. Still, they give the Club all the attention they can. Minutes of the period reveal the awareness of a number of sociological changes which altered the nature of the work, making it more difficult for these leaders. Amongst the difficulties they faced was a factor noted at a meeting of the Board on April 6, 1989, namely that Inverness churches had generally become more "isolationist" with regard to their young people taking part in outside clubs like the YMCA; also, it appeared to the Board that young people had largely become "consumers" rather than "participators" in voluntary activities such as those conducted through the YMCA. These fundamental changes meant that leaders in Inverness YMCA of the eighties and nineties faced different (and, humanly speaking, probably more difficult) challenges than their predecessors.

But God is the same; "I am the Lord, I change not!" And the spiritual needs of young people are the same; "He that hath not the Son of God hath not life!" And the Gospel is the same; "... the Gospel of Christ (which) is the power of God unto salvation unto all that believe!" So, God's work at Inverness YMCA goes on, adjusting itself to today's needs methodologically, but "holding fast the Word of life," Scripturally and theologically.

Like earlier leaders, the Board of Management supported a wide range of Club activities to reach Inverness youth. There were films on Hogmanay night and a sleep-over at the Club (which, for some boys, if it did nothing else, kept them from a riotous night of excess in their own home); there was a Photographic Club, Table Tennis and Badminton tournaments (these latter being led by Mr. Joe Lafferty); billiards and snooker, darts and table games. As well, there was all the preparation required for what had now become an annual fund-raising Sale of Work to augment the members' and friends' contributions, and outside donations such as the greatly-appreciated annual gift provided by the Hector Russell Trust administered through the office of Mr Caldwell.

In 1979, a trip to Germany was sponsored by the YMCA. The

group planned to spend one week in Munich and one week in a Hostel in Bavaria. Since the cost per person was 110 pounds, it was proposed that a 20 pound grant be given to each 16-25 year old member planning to take the trip.

The Board members took turns opening the Club each evening. Two new ventures included a Thursday night prayer meeting and the alteration of the Sunday Evening format.

In 1985, one man, Thomas Mackay, pressed the Board firmly for more personal work to be done through the Club and ended up heading an Evangelism Outreach 'Ways and Means' committee.

At the time of writing (Autumn, 1992) Inverness YMCA continues a programme of ministry to young men. Two Club meetings each week conclude with a short Bible study; young men like David Roberts and David Summers are active in these meetings, along with local church youth leaders such as Alister MacInnes and many others.

As well as the leaders already mentioned, the general secretary' position is well-filled by Ian MacDonald who, with his wife, is a full-time worker in the Young Women's Christians Association. Another valued worker is Ali Paul who, with his wife's help, painted the entire Club. Ali also takes an interest in the scheduled activities.

There are occasional YMCA-sponsored summer camping activities; and the Sunday Evening After Church Rally, that meeting through which God has been pleased to bless many down through the years, still functions as a meeting place for YMCA members and friends to worship together in a fellowship which includes but transcends local church distinctives.

However, change is in the air. Present Board leaders, committed and willing, are praying for God to raise up younger men who will take the baton, carry the torch, bear the flag to their own generation of youth.

Let all friends and supporters of Inverness YMCA join in this prayer, that God will continue to bless in every way, the work He himself commenced through five Inverness men almost a century and a half ago.

The YMCA in Jerusalem.

Garden of Gethsename with the oldest olive trees in the world.

Chapter Twenty-Eight

From Mud Hut to the Hilton Hotel

We close our anecdotal acount of Inverness YMCA by returning to Wilfred Urquhart.

In 1973, Wilfred left Scotland for Upper Volta (This country is now known as Burkino Faso.) The pilgrimage which had its beginning when Wilfred bowed his head under the sheet and gave his heart to the Lord in Inverness some fifteen years before had matured Wilf from a callow Christian to a mature missionary candidate. Now, having completed his years of training, including the acquisition of the French language, he was on his way to replace Bryan Woodward in Malba.

When he arrived, Wilfred found something waiting for his use. It was the very Land Rover which his financial contributions had helped to buy some years before.

Some time after Wilf's arrival in Malba, WEC headquarters were requested to obtain and send out a power-winch for the Land Rover. It was an essential piece of equipment as the vehicle often bogged down in the muddy tracks and required its own equipment to pull itself out.

Somehow, responsibility for that Land Rover had become so intertwined with Inverness YMCA and its interest in Wilf that, when a husband and wife team of WEC representatives came to Inverness, Keith Martin took them to Tom MacDonald's place of employment. The couple were searching for a winch for the Land Rover. From there, they went to French's Electricians, where they saw a rusty old winch half-buried in the yard where it had lay disused for years. The yard man was a bit indifferent to the WEC couple's inquiries, but phoned their request to his manager in his Nairn office, fifteen miles away.

"From WEC?" The manager responded. "Polish that winch up right away and give it to them. No charge!"

Only a suitable packing box was needed now to transport the item to Africa. African customs required the part to be packed in its original container. That seemed impossible but, back at Tom's workplace, the premises were searched for a suitable box.

"Look at this!" Tom's tone was a mixture of amazement and awe. Stuck away in a corner of the plant, filled with junk, was the original factory-made wooden box with the very part numbers for the winch which the WEC man held in his hand. Nobody knew how the box ever got there. It had been there for years. But everybody knew Who it was that regarded the lowly need of His servants and proved His interest in their small affairs. "Before they call, I will answer."

Mr. Wesley Affleck of Winnipeg Bible College used to say, "God is great in great things; but God is very great in little things." The provision of the winch was miracle enough. The added extra of the very factory box to transport it was overwhelming.

Wilfred spent his first two years in Upper Volta learning the Birifor language as a prerequisite to ministering among the native people. In Easter, 1975, he was struck down with hepatitis.

Being seven hundred miles from outside help, Wilfred could only lie in his native-built hut, completely without strength and helpless even to care for his own most basic needs. The primitive sanitary conditions in his native village setting represented a high risk for anybody with such an ailment. The German lady doctor who tended him finally laid down the ultimatum. "Go home. If you stay here two more weeks, you will go home in a coffin."

A few days before, Inverness YMCA had mailed support money for Wilf in the usual manner. The money, however, arrived exactly when needed to procure Wilfred's plane fare.

Wilfred was so ill he hardly remembers anything of the flight in the single-engine Cessna, nor being taken aboard the large jet to fly from the nation's capital to Paris, France for his connection to London.

When he arrived at Paris, Wilfred learned that his plane had landed too late for him to make his connection. The airline person was amazed at the equanimity with which Wilf received the news. "Aren't you annoyed?" she asked with some surprise. "Not at all," Wilf replied.

The airline company put Wilf up in the Hilton Hotel near Orly Airport. Far too ill to enjoy the unfamiliar luxury, Wilf phoned Donald Graham who attended a Bible School outside Paris. The two met next morning, Donald benefiting from Wilf's illness by being able to scoff the sumptuous Hilton hotel breakfast which Wilfred was too sick to eat.

From Paris, Wilf flew to London and became an outpatient at the MildMay Mission Hospital. Living at WEC London headquarters, Wilf renewed acquaintance with a girl who had been a first year student during Wilf's second year of training. Pat Clark, a Scottish girl from Stanley, Perthshire, had just returned from a one year term teaching position at a mission school in Senegal and was at WEC headquarters seeking the Lord's will for her. She and Wilf met in the corridor and talked for hours, Wilf catching up on the news of their mutual friends and fellow-students; and Pat hearing all about life in Upper Volta.

It was a pleasant friendship, that was all. Both Wilf and Pat, in true WEC tradition, were committed only to what the Lord desired. Neither would deliberately advance a special relationship without the Lord's direct leading. But it was nice to have a friend, be a friend, walk together, talk together, pray together.

"We took part in a prayer battery at WEC headquarters." Pat later told the story. "I played the piano for the hymn-singing, then sat at the piano while another missionary, Jordan Khun, spoke. I had a great hunger to know what God wanted me to do. "God, I have to know, tonight," was my heart's cry. Suddenly, and unexpectedly, I heard a voice - an audible voice. I can only say now that I know I heard it, though I'd never had such an experience before nor have I had since. The voice said, "You are going to Upper Volta with Wilf."

Even now, when Pat narrates the story, she remembers the confusion this revelation brought to her. She certainly could not tell Wilf. God, Who evidently had shown her, must also show him.

Wilf, meanwhile, was going through a dark period of confusion. After all the preparation, after all the language study, why was he not in Africa? The question beat on his heart but no answer came. Discharged from MildMay hospital, Wilf went up to Inverness where he continued the voice therapy which had been made necessary by his illness.

"I needed a tape recorder from headquarters, and I knew Pat was coming to Scotland," Wilf recalled. "So I wrote asking her to bring the recorder to Glasgow where I would meet her."

When the couple met they discovered their conversation deepened into shared questions about God's plan for their future. As the implications became clear, Wilf and Pat reconsecrated themselves to God and agreed not to communicate with each other in any way for the next ten days. The time would be dedicated to prayer. If God gave both of them an unmistakeable assurance that He wanted them to serve Him together as man and wife, their relationship would proceed. If God gave no such assurance, or gave it to only one, but not the other, the relationship would end.

Back in Inverness, on the ninth day, Wilf cried to the Lord

for an answer - and the answer came. It was from 2 Corinthians 5:18 and it filled Wilf's heart with the assurance he sought. The words were, 'All things are of God.' In a moment of revelation, Wilf's joy overflowed as he understood the will of the Lord. But, it was a word that had to be confirmed by Pat's experience, too. Dashing off a letter which he knew would reach her on the tenth day, Wilf waited on God to bring the outcome.

In the meantime, Pat also sought the Lord. Not doubting the word she had received at the headquarters prayer meeting, Pat still felt it necessary to plead for confirmation in light of the agreement she and Wilf had made. Again God spoke, this time from Job 22:21. "Acquaint thyself with Him and be at peace," was the clinching word. And peace it was that Pat experienced as she received Wilf's letter and quickly phoned him to tell him of God's Word to her.

Curiously, the WEC leaders with whom Wilf and Pat consulted about becoming man and wife were not completely surprised. They readily gave their blessing to the two honest young servants of God who stood before them. Wilf and Pat were married in Easter, 1976 and took up ministry in Upper Volta in October of the same year.

"Inverness YMCA continued to share a vital part of our ministry," Wilf acknowledged. "They sent us an annual gift of between six and eight hundred pounds to support us in our work. More importantly, we knew that our friends in Inverness YMCA prayed for us constantly."

At the time of writing, Wilf and Pat have temporarily relocated from their ministry in Upper Volta to serve the Lord in Kilcreggan, Scotland, WEC's Conference Centre where missionary outreach is emphasized. The Urquharts have two children, Robert and Andrew, whose educational needs dictated a time away from Upper Volta. The Urquharts keep in contact with Inverness YMCA, Wilf's spiritual birthplace - and the Inverness YMCA keep in contact with them. Whether serving the Lord in Kilcreggan, or in Africa, Wilf is a representative of the Lord Who saved and commissioned him - and one of many representatives of the Inverness YMCA which, though centred in the Highlands of Scotland has, by God's grace, been permitted to spread its influence through three half-centuries and across the earth.

Wilf's story has been told throughout this anecdotal history, because Wilf's story represents the values and goals and priorities which have permeated Inverness YMCA in the past and continue to guide it in the present. For Wilf's conversion, spiritual growth, and missionary service, and indeed, for all those who have been saved, built up spiritually, and sent forth into God's service from Inverness, YMCA, we give thanks, and all the glory, to God.

Group of Members in 1991. Front row — some of the new leaders — Andrew Wilson, Ian MacDonald, David Summers, David Roberts, Derek Fraser.

Appendix

*List of Principal Stallholders at YMCA Sales of
Work and Coffee Mornings.*

Mrs. Minnie Anderson
Mrs. Catherine Chambers
Mrs. Ruth Finlay
Mrs. A. Hamilton
Mrs. Dorothy MacEwen
Miss Marion MacEwen
Mrs. Florrie MacKenzie
Mrs. Joan MacKenzie
Mrs. Peggy MacKenzie
Mrs. Mary MacLean
Mrs. T. Paterson
Mrs. Muriel Pearson
Mrs. Isabel Ross
Mrs. C. Ross
Miss Mary Shaw
Mrs. Anne Sutherland
Mrs. Eilean Sutherland
Mrs. Chrissie Williamson
Miss Florence Williamson
Miss Margaret Williamson
Miss Norma Mackenzie
and
the many others.